Jean-Baptiste Morin

Astrologia Gallica

Book Twenty-Six

Astrological Interrogations and Elections

Translated from the Latin
by
James Herschel Holden, M.A.
Fellow of the American Federation of
Astrologers

Copyright 2010 by James Herschel Holden

No part of this book may be reproduced or transcribed in any form or by any means, electronic or mechanical, including photocopying or recording, or by any information storage and retrieval system without written permission from the author and publisher, except in the case of brief quotations embodied in critical reviews and articles. Requests and inquiries may be mailed to: American Federation of Astrologers, Inc., P.O. Box 22040, Tempe, AZ 85283.

First Printing 2010

ISBN-10: 0-86690-608-8
ISBN-13: 978-0-86690-608-1

Published by:
American Federation of Astrologers, Inc.
6535 S. Rural Road
Tempe, AZ 85283

www.astrologers.com

Printed in the United States of America.

This book is dedicated to the memory of
Douglas Alexander Kidd,
whose book has helped me much.

TABLE OF CONTENTS

Translator's Preface   vii

Book Twenty-Six
Section I. Astrological Interrogations

Chapter 1. What the Doctrine of Interrogations Involves and what the Limits of its Truth are   5

Chapter 2. Whether the celestial bodies are Causes per se of all Man's Actions and Motions   6

Chapter 3. Whether the Beginnings of all things are like the Birth of a Man   9

Chapter 4. The Doctrine of the Arabs on Interrogations Depends upon many vain Assumptions   14

Chapter 5. The Doctrine of the Arabs on Interrogations is Plainly False   20

Chapter 6. The Doctrine of the Arabs on Questions is Fraudulent   30

Chapter 7. The Doctrine of the Arabs on Interrogations is Diabolical   31

Chapter 8. The Falsity of the Responses to Interrogations from the Ruler of the Planetary Hour   32

Chapter 9. Containing Cardan's Errors in his Tract on Interrogations   38

Chapter 10. To how many General Categories can all the Questions put to an Astrologer be Reduced   43

Chapter 11. In what General Way should Judgment be made on the Questions Pertaining to those Six Categories   45

v

Section II. Astrological elections

Chapter 1. What the Doctrine of Astrological Elections Involves and what the Limits of its Truth are	51
Chapter 2. Some things to be Generally Noted Concerning Elections	52
Chapter 3. How Great the Utility of the Doctrine of Elections is	55
Chapter 4. How Vain the Arguments of Alexander de Angelis Against Elections are	61
Chapter 5. What Cardan Thought about Elections	66
Chapter 6. General Rules Necessary for Elections. And in what Way an Election Should be Made for any Particular Thing	69
Chapter 7. In which the Use of Elections is Shown and Proved by two Notable Examples	78
Appendix 1. The Equation of Time	95
Index of Persons	97
Bibliography	101

Translator's Preface

In this, the last Book of the *Astrologia Gallica*, Morin takes up the subject of *Interrogations* and *Elections*. Section I deals with Interrogations, which are the subject of what is now called *Horary Astrology*, i.e. the art of judging a chart set for the moment when someone (technically called the *Querent*) proposes a *Question* and asks an astrologer to give him information about the present state of the matter and its likely outcome. This is an ancient part of astrology, but Morin did not know that. He had read Ptolemy's *Tetrabiblos* and Firmicus Maternus's *Mathesis*, neither of which says anything about Interrogations; consequently, he assumed that Horary Astrology was something that the Arabs had invented during the Middle Ages.

And since from his point of view the Arabs were infidels and followers of a false religion, their invention was obviously worthless and ungodly (in fact he ascribes it to the Devil). He therefore devotes the first 9 Chapters of Section I to proving (to his own satisfaction) that Horary Astrology is merely a silly business based on a foolish notion of the Arabs. He even devotes an entire Chapter to denouncing the validity and use of Planetary Hours as a particularly egregious example of Arabian foolishness—being unaware that they were a part of Greek astrology from its earliest days.

And he repeatedly levies the charge that all astrologers who erect and read Horary charts for Clients are practicing a valueless and fraudulent art merely for profit.[1]

---

[1] Some modern English astrologers have expressed the same opinion, among them A. J. Pearce (1840-1923) and Alan Leo (1860-1917). But most astrologers today either practice Horary Astrology or have no quarrel with it.

But what Morin did not know was that Horary Astrology under the original name *Catarchic Astrology* (which included both Horary and Elections) goes back at least to the first century A.D. and probably to the Alexandrian inventors of Horoscopic Astrology before that. It was certainly a Greek science, not one invented by the Arabs. And even if it had been an Arab invention, Morin is inconsistent in dismissing it for that reason, for elsewhere in the *Astrologia Gallica* he makes constant use of Solar and Lunar Revolutions (Returns), which were also inventions of the Arabs. But he may have supposed that they were invented by some Western astrologer.

He also seems to think that Horary Astrology is somehow in conflict with Free Will. And since he was a devout Catholic, he was obliged in all his theoretical considerations to maintain that astrology was not inconsistent with Free Will.

And it does not seem to have occurred to him that a Natal Horoscope can also be considered to be a Horary chart set for a time certain (the birth time), for which the question is, "What are the characteristics of this person, and what will befall him in the future." And while (in Section II) he looks with restricted favor on Elections, again it does not seem to have occurred to him that an Election chart is a Horary chart set for a time certain in the future, for which the question is, "What will the attendant circumstances be at that time, and what will be the outcome?"

To make matters worse, Morin's other favorite types of chart, the Solar Revolution and the Lunar Revolution, are also Horary charts set for times certain, for which the question is, "How will things be for this person during this time period, and what significant events will happen to him?"

Curiously too, the "Morin method" of interpreting a chart follows the standard Horary method of *accidental* significators rather than the Ptolemaic method of *general* significators. But Morin does not seem to have recognized that fact.

However, in the last two chapters of Section I, Morin first lists six different types of Questions that may occur, and then gives rules for judging them by using natal charts and their directions and revolutions, and even extracted charts.[1] And for Mundane Questions he recommends being guided by the natal charts of the prominent persons involved and by universal constitutions and their directions, etc. But once or twice he mentions setting a chart for a time certain just as a Horary chart would have been set, but he instructs the reader to interpret it with careful regard to the natal charts, etc.

Aside from all this, it is plain that Morin's objections to Horary Astrology are based on various theoretical considerations, not on personal experience! For example in Section I, Chapter 5, he asserts that if the same question is asked several times, the several charts will differ, so that no true answer can be forthcoming. This immediately betrays a lack of experience. For if a question is asked when the Querent is seriously motivated to ask the question, Astrologers have found that the chart will give a true indication, whether it is the first and only time the question is asked or one of several subsequent times.[2]

It is a pity that Morin was unable to read English, for in 1647 his younger contemporary across the Channel, the great English Astrologer William Lilly (1602-1681) published an elaborate treatise on Horary Astrology as the second section of his book *Christian Astrology* (London: Partridge and Blunden, 1647). Lilly not only sets forth rules for judging various types of Horary questions, but he illustrates the application of the rules with two dozen example charts and commentaries, thus proving the efficacy of Horary Astrology by actual experimentation. This contrasts strongly with

---

[1]He accepted these because they are mentioned by Ptolemy in his *Tetrabiblos*.
[2]I speak from personal experience. Many years ago, over a period of nearly a decade, perhaps thirty times or more a question arose in my mind as to whether a certain event would ever take place. Each time, I erected a Horary chart. There are four basic ways that a Horary chart can return a "No" answer. In every instance, one or the other of those negatives appeared in the chart. And the often repeated "No" answer was correct, for the questioned event never occurred!

ix

Morin's Book 26, in which he gives no examples to prove that Horary Astrology doesn't work, but merely presents a long-winded denunciation of it based solely on theoretical assumptions and an incorrect view of astrological history.

In the Second Part of Book 26, the Section on Elections, Morin discusses an important theoretical restriction for Elections. Since he assumes that the major circumstances and events of a person's life are signified by his natal chart, and its primary directions and revolutions, then obviously an Election cannot override or significantly alter those indications. Hence, if an Election is chosen for an action and a time that does not conform to those fundamental indications, it cannot give the desired result. That is, the chosen Election cannot indicate an outcome that does not conform to the fundamental indications in force at that time. This would seem to restrict the use of Elections to choosing a particular time within a time period already indicative of a particular type of event. And this would be a definite limitation on the use of Elections! However in Chapter 6 he gives an extensive set of rules for making Elections, taking those restrictions into account.

Further on, however, as practical examples of properly chosen Elections, Morin inserts several charts in this section of the book that are set for the times at which important incidents occurred in the life of a prominent French government official. He begins with an Election he made for the start of a lengthy journey planned by the Client for the spring of 1646; and another Election that he made later to select the time for starting the return from that journey. Finally, he made an Election to select a favorable time for a meeting between his Client and the French Prime Minister. In the associated discussions, reference is constantly made to natal horoscopes and to solar and lunar revolutions (returns) in the Client's nativity and also (for the journey) in Morin's own nativity since Morin accompanied the Client on the journey. And Morin explains how things turned out after each Election. After which, Morin concludes Book 26 by saying that he could include many more charts of Elections from his own practice, but he thinks that the ones he has shown are sufficient to demonstrate the utility of Elections when they are made according to his rules.

The Reader who takes up this book without having read the translations of the earlier Books of the *Astrologia Gallica* (and particularly Book 21), will no doubt find it hard reading. He may then wonder if the translation was properly made. I can assure him that the Latin text is more difficult to understand than the translation, and that without resorting to unrestricted paraphrase it would be difficult to render it into easy English. Morin had a thorough command of Latin and had learned to write what are called "periodic sentences." These are sentences that go on and on with many clauses and sometimes with the main verb in the middle or at the end. (Those who have struggled to decipher Cicero's speeches to the Senate in Third Year Latin will know what I mean.)

I have occasionally broken those long sentences up into two or more parts, but usually I have kept them together with a liberal use of commas, semi-colons and dashes. I have also added words in brackets here and there, and I have added some explanatory footnotes to make the translation more understandable. Still, the result is not always easy to read, and the Reader who wants to understand what Morin is trying to impart to him will occasionally find some sentences that he will have to re-read and think about. I believe that if he does that, he will understand them, and he will be glad that he took the trouble to do so.

The charts shown in this translation are facsimiles of the charts in Book 26 of the *Astrologia Gallica* and are therefore in the old square form. The Reader should note that in the center of the charts the day of the month and the time in hours are given, both reckoned from the preceding noon. I have given the date and time reckoned from the previous midnight below some of the charts. The times are all stated in Local Apparent Time. If the Reader wishes to recalculate the charts with a modern computer, he may need to convert the time in LAT to the equivalent time in Local Mean Time. This can easily be done by reference to the Equation of Time

xi

table in Appendix 1.

Finally, I would like to emphasize what I said earlier: The basic outline of Morin's method of interpretation is set forth in *Astrologia Gallica,* Book 21, but the amplifying details and many examples are in Books 13-20 and 22-25 of the *Astrologia Gallica.* The Reader who tries to learn the Morin method by reading only one or two of those books will not acquire the whole method but only pieces of it. The method itself is straightforward in theory but complicated in details. Admittedly, reading thirteen books to learn how to interpret one chart or predict one event may seem to be both daunting and excessively demanding. But the diligent Reader's patience will be rewarded.

James H. Holden
Phoenix, Arizona
18 July 2010

ASTROLOGIA GALLICA

BOOK TWENTY-SIX

ASTROLOGICAL INTERROGATIONS AND ELECTIONS

PREFACE

Not without reason, this Book deserves to have the last place in our Natal Astrology. for it adds something astrological to the prior Books; and especially to the erections of Radix Charts and those of Revolutions, and their Directions and the Transits of the planets through the conformable places of the Charts, without the inspection of which the Astrologer will only by chance respond with the truth to Questions asked or elect a suitable time for undertaking a thing because he would certainly be ignorant of both. Moreover, it cannot be expressed in a few words of how great a moment these things are, but it can be proved by very frequent experiments. But actually no one has hitherto expunged this doctrine from figments and errors and handed down its true foundations. But almost all the astrologers, and especially the Arabs and the Indians[1] *have abused them for the sake of their own profit in a notable disgrace to Astrology and the frequent ruin of those who have consulted Astrologers of that sort. Since, moreover, it is very necessary in directing one's life to avoid evils and to procure particular good things at appropriate times, it is therefore very useful; indeed, almost all the fruit of Astrology can be collected from it; therefore, in this Book we have taken particular care to hand down in their purity both doctrines, namely that of Interrogations and of Elections. Whether we have done that, the fair-minded Reader will judge.*

---

[1] Unfortunately, Morin was under the false impression that Horary Astrology was something invented by the Arabs because there is no mention of it in Ptolemy's *Tetrabiblos*, nor does Firmicus say anything about it in the *Mathesis*. And since the Arabs, from Morin's point of view were followers of a false religion, there were two reasons to discount their treatises on Horary Astrology.

SECTION I.
Astrological Interrogations.

Chapter 1. *Concerning the Doctrine of Interrogations and what are the Limits of its Truth.*

The doctrine of astrological interrogations is concerned with true responses made by an astrologer to questions propounded to him about past, present, or future things. Moreover, Haly[1] says, in the first part of his *Judgments of the Stars*, Chapter 5, that Ptolemy has dismissed this doctrine as a false one, which Cardan also states at the end of his *Quadripartite*, Book 4, Chapter 10, where he says, that this doctrine is one of fortune-telling; but afterwards, he composed a *Treatise on Interrogations*, which he mentioned at the end of his *Commentary on the Quadripartite*.

But Haly, along with Vuellius,[2] and other Arabs, embraced it as true, and he handed down in the first, second, and third part of his *Judgments of the Stars*, to which he added the *Book of the Nine Judges*,[3] where astrology regarding questions of whatever kind is treated with a hitherto unrestrained license, no consideration being had of the natal figure, as with a question made about a thief, not only in particular what was stolen, where [the thief] has fled, where in fact he is, but also of his appearance, age, and religion, how many letters his name consists of, which ones they are, and how the thief's name is compounded of them, such things the as-

---

[1] ʿAlî ibn abi 'r-Rijâl (11th century). His extensive manual of astrology is called *Liber completus de iudiciis astrorum* 'The Complete Book on the Judgments of the Stars' (Venice: Erhard Ratdolt, 1485).

[2] This is actually the second century Greek astrologer Vettius Valens, who is quoted in some of the Arabic astrology books. Morin evidently thought that he was an Arab.

[3] According to Francis Carmody, *Arabic Astronomical and Astrological Sciences in Latin Translation* (Berkeley and Los Angeles: University of California Press, 1956), the Basel edition of 1571 has *The Book of Nine Judges II* at the end of Haly's book; but it was not part of Haly's book. There are two books entitled *Liber novem iudicum* 'The Book of Nine Judges'. The second of these was printed at Venice by Peter Liechtenstein in 1509, and reprinted with Haly's book.

trologers stupidly presume to define, asserting that either there is truth in all these, or it is not in the figures of the nativities; indeed, because they want not only the nativities of men, but also all their actions, thoughts, and questions to be due to celestial causes.

But I, having avoided both the last opinions, namely [those] of Ptolemy and those Arabs, think that I should walk in the middle, and that I should speak, not to anything at all, but only to other questions, [that is, to whether] the astrologers are able to give true responses, namely to those which are made for persons whose figure of nativity is had, and from the things signified in that figure, from the consideration of which those same responses are deduced.

Chapter 2. *Whether the Celestial Bodies are Causes per se of all the Actions and Motions of Man.*

This to be sure is not only supposed, but also asserted by the Arabs and the other astrologers, who undertake to judge about anything asked, solely from a celestial chart erected for the moment of the question. For Omar[1] speaks about this in [his Book] *Of Judgments*, Chapter 9:

> "That the divine force and motion of the celestial circle at the hour of that question compels the querent to ask. For the human condition does not cease to imitate the effects of both the celestial circles and those of the stars, [and] their order and progress, due to some as it were bond of love."

Therefore, they will have it that the stars move the Querent under the celestial constitution, which is conformable to the desired truth.

---

[1]The reference is to Omar Tiberiades (d. c. 815/816), who wrote a book entitled *De nativitatibus* 'Nativities' (Venice: Sessa, 1503) and another entitled *De iudiciis astrorum* 'The Judgments of the Stars'. There are also citations from his books in *Liber novum iudicum* (Venice: Peter Lichtenstein, 1509).

Besides, that is said by the astrologers of that sect, but it is neither proved, nor can it be proved; for in fact, because this opinion introduces fated necessity, which also Ptolemy himself, a heathen man, in *Quadripartite*, Book 1, Chapter 2, disproves very nicely. And we, in Book 23, Chapter 16, have proved that of those things that happen to the native from natural causes, some are effectively from the stars alone, others solely from his own will; some solely from other sublunar causes, but some from the common course of these causes; and it is false to assert that everything that naturally happens to a man [arises] from celestial causes alone.

And that is clearly confirmed by this: because if the present constitution of the *Caelum* should move me to anger or extravagance, since, by the common consensus of all those who grant free will to man, this motion is not inevitable, to be sure it is certain that through my free will I can resist the celestial motion; and if I resist, that it is not from the present celestial constitution, which if from predominance may move the passions of the mind to wrath or extravagance, will it not also at the same time move [me] to resist those same passions, or move [me] to opposite virtues; but it is from my own will, which is per se not subject to the stars, since it is of a superior nature, because of its being spiritual. For that reason therefore, it is entirely false to assert that the celestial bodies per se are the causes of all the actions, thoughts, and motions of man.

Besides, when Omar says *"that the force of the circle is divine and its motion at the hour of the question compels the Querent to ask,"* he calls forth against himself the Indians and those of Ferith[1] and Babylon, who assert that the questions propounded are by the will of the Querent. And this, therefore, is true, because since man is free in his own nature, he cannot be compelled by the stars to propound a question; and although he might conceive it, he will nevertheless not propound it unless he wants to. And it is this that greatly disturbs those who profess this vanity, who cannot agree

---
[1] Probably Persia.

among themselves, at what moment the figure ought to be erected by the astrologer [to obtain] a response.

For Hermes and Vuellius[1] in Haly, Part 10, Chapter 7, will not have it:

> "that the hour of taking the ASC is that moment in which the Querent comes to the master or the astrologer. Haly himself will have it that the hour of taking the ASC of the question is that moment in which the Querent bids the astrologer to take the ASC, that is to erect the figure: for (he says) if he comes and does not say that he should take the ASC, that is not the ASC, unless he says when [to take it]."

From which it is plain that Haly agrees with the Indians and the Babylonians in this, because the question and its ASC are put within the will of the Querent. And consequently, the stars do not move and determine the question, but on the contrary it determines the celestial figure at its own pleasure.

But if some quibbler says that in that moment in which the Querent asks the astrologer, in that same moment the figure of the *Caelum*, containing the truth of the thing quesited, moves that same Querent to ask his question, as Omar would have it, I respond **first**: here the beginning is to be sought, and it must be proved that the figure of the *Caelum* always contains the truth of the thing quesited at the moment in which the Querent asks the astrologer. I reply **second**: either the querent can retard the question or he cannot; if the latter is the case, he is compelled and his freedom is taken away, which it is wicked to assert; if the former is the case, then either there will be no truth in the response or it will be only hypothetical. Certainly, because if he now propounds a question, this will be the truth of the response, but if after one or two hours, there will be another truth of the response, whence the vanity of this art is manifestly plain.

---

[1] Vettius Valens, as noted above.

It can be said more subtly, because at the moment in which he thinks of something concerning any truth that is to be sought from an astrologer, then the figure containing the truth of the *Caelum* moves him, and therefore the figure ought to be erected at that moment. True, except that the astrologers do not accept that, lest they may seem unsure about the true figure, on account of the uncertainty [of the time] of that moment. It does not suffice to think about propounding a question, for a casual thought quickly vanishes; but in the case of anxiety, a man will reflect for a long time on whether he should approach an astrologer or not before he decides on one or the other [course]; and if he decides to go to an astrologer, at the moment of his decision the figure should rather be erected; but always, as I said previously, he could either delay his decision or not, and either way, it would be absurd.

Chapter 3. *Whether the Beginnings of all Things are like the Birth of a Man.*

Haly, in Part 1, chapter 5, along with Hermes, Vuellius, and the other Arabs, in order to establish their own art of questions, assert that the beginnings of all things, either [those that are] natural, such as a man, a horse; or something artificial, such as a house, a statue; or something corporeal, such as a battle; or something spiritual, such as a thought, a question, a speech, etc., are like the birth of a man, and since they are caused by the *Caelum*, consequently a judgment can be made about them individually as about the birth of a man.

And because it cannot be done, as if his own nativity and its annual revolution signified marriage to anyone, or misfortune on a journey, that same thing would not appear in a question, because no hour can have a signification unless it is in accord with the nativity and the revolution of the year, and because if anything of these is false, they are all false. These things that are asserted no less falsely than imprudently—in short without any reason or proof—are removed from the true science of astrology for the following reasons.

First. Only the seminal spirit of things in general is the proper subject for the infusion of the influx of the celestial bodies, as was shown by us in Book 12, Chapters 11 and 29, and in Book 20, Section 4. But all artifacts are lacking in seed; and therefore the celestial bodies do not act influentially on them, as was abundantly proved in Book 20, Section 4, Chapter 8. Much less do battles, thoughts, questions, speeches, and things similar to them have any seed by which they are physically generated; therefore, none of those are subject per se to celestial influences.

Second. When anyone proposes a question to an astrologer, the celestial influx is imprinted either upon the Querent, or the astrologer, or on the question itself, or upon the thing asked about; but none of these can be affected. For it is not imprinted on the Querent himself at the moment of the question; otherwise, it would follow that the *Caelum* in its own influx or action would depend upon the will of the Querent, namely in whose will it is to propose the question, or not to propose it, or to delay it by choice; and so the *Caelum* is not acting naturally, namely because it cannot by itself restrain its own effect; but it always acts according to its proper force due to the necessity of nature; or it at least follows the will to assign to the *Caelum* by choice the force of signifying the quesited truth—which things are plainly absurd!

The same logic is appropriate for the astrologer, then for the question itself, about which it can truly be said that it does not have its beginning or its existence per se from the *Caelum*, but only from the free will of the Querent. And finally it is true for the thing about which the question is made, which generally will not be more ample, as when it is a question about a man, whether he is alive, who nevertheless is [already] dead. Therefore, from these things it is plain how great the difference is between a man being born, on whom the *Caelum* necessarily acts, and independently of the will of any man, and a question that is made, and the other things mentioned above; and in consequence, how great is the foolishness of this art!

Third. If in the instant when a question is proposed, there would be any impression from the *Caelum*, this would be upon the question which then begins to be in existence, not otherwise, and they will have the house in which moment it begins to receive an influential impression from the *Caelum*; and consequently it would be necessary to judge, not about the thing quesited, but about the question itself, examining it by the signification of the 12 houses, just as Haly, in that same Part 1, chapter 6, tried to accommodate those things to all the things whose beginnings are proposed for the astrologer to look at. He says:

> "that the ASC or the first house is the significator of the property of the thing. The second [house] is the significator of the price of the thing. The third, what happens in the thing, and what is adjoined to itself in one kind. The fourth signifies the offspring of the thing and its roots. The fifth signifies the condition of the thing and that which is generated by it. The sixth signifies the durability of the things and that which serves it. The seventh signifies the contrary of the thing in that same strength existing from its offspring. The eighth signifies the vile estimation of the things, its end and diminution. The ninth signifies the removal of the thing, and the causes that are attached to it. The tenth signifies the nobility and the excellence of the thing and its peculiarity in things done. The eleventh signifies the complement of the thing, its beauty and convenience. The twelfth signifies the diversity of things and the bad accidents that happen to it. Whence, [if] the ruler of that house of those already mentioned is in a good state, the nature of that thing is directed according to the amount of reason and the advancement of the ruler of that one."

These things of Haly, and neither [anything else from] Haly, nor from the rest of the Arabs, answer any of the above said things about that question, on which they cannot even agree, as is plain per se; but they respond with those same things concerning the thing about which there is a question, why occasionally those things also agree to some small degree, and in which that celestial impression does not fall, since very often it doesn't – as when there is a question about some past matter, or about some future matter, or about a man, whether he may live, who is already dead.

Some will perhaps say that the celestial influx is not indeed imprinted upon any of the 4 things mentioned above—namely the Querent, the astrologer, the question, or the thing about which the there is a question—as was proved above, but rather upon the celestial figure, or its state at the moment of the question, to contain in its own signification the truth of that question.

But I respond **first**. The *Caelum*, therefore, does not move the Querent, as is commonly stated, for that motion cannot be conceived by the Querent without a received influx. And then I should say that the state of the *Caelum* either has that signification always, or only when there is a question. If the former [is true], there will consequently be no need to bother about the time, nor about one [particular] figure or another For from any one of them the same truth of the question can be elicited against the opinion of the Arabs and the principles of this art. If the **second** [is true], it will, therefore, only have that signification from the will of the Querent, which has already been very often rejected. Therefore, it is plain in all ways that this doctrine of the Arabs is entirely false.

But if anyone will object to the erection of celestial figures at the beginning of illnesses with the approval of the Church of Rome, which it has never abandoned for [use in] medicine, I reply: illnesses arise through natural generation from their own seeds, and they have their own symptoms, motion, and periods, as well as natural beginnings; but questions lack seeds and have only arbitrary beginnings, which is a great disparity; therefore, illnesses are produced by the stars, but questions are not, and the figures of illnesses contain truth, but the figures of questions do not.

Much more seriously it will follow that if anyone will object that by our reasons the doctrine of nativities can be overturned, for if the native receives from the stars an influx for an ambition [to achieve] dignities. When he seeks or buys a dignity (which is going to be offered for sale in France, Oh horror and shame!), either he is moved by the *Caelum*, or he is not. If he is not moved, then it is said in vain that an influx from the stars for a desire for dignities has been received in the nativity; [but] if he is moved, then either the *Caelum* always has the strength to move the native thus, or only when he himself seeks or buys a dignity.

If you say this, since it is a fact that to seek or to buy depends on the native's free will; therefore, the *Caelum* will not have that force on its part, but it will be from the native's will; consequently, the native will not be moved by the *Caelum*—contrary to the hypothesis—when he does not want to move, unless it should first have the strength to move him. If you said that it was on the part of the *Caelum*, then no reason will be given why the native seeks today rather than previously or later.

But I reply that when the native seeks or buys a dignity on account of an influx for the ambition [for] dignities received from the stars in his nativity, then he is moved by the *Caelum* through its radical influx, a conformable radical direction, and conformable revolutions of the Sun and the Moon and their directions, as well as by conformable transits, all of which—or the greater part of them—occur together, at which time he is moved for the act, but not always; therefore, the *Caelum* does not always have such a power of moving, as has been explained by us more fully in its own places.

And he does not receive the power of moving from his own will, in which to be sure there is neither the power to be moved or not to be moved—at least naturally—but only to seek or not to seek, seeing that from the doctrine repeated by us in many places, the will in its own proper actions is not subject to the stars, but it can only resist their motion, so that it is not allotted their own [full] effect, not only at one hour or one day, but also altogether; although it cannot escape that motion—at least naturally—because that motion is a natural one.

Besides, the time of seeking also has some latitude through the transits, which are the causes of all things, especially particular ones, and those things of shorter duration for actually moving [the event]. For the search or the purchase can by common consensus be known not only on the very day of a partile transit, but on the day before, or the day after, unless it was a transit of the Moon; indeed, the whole time of application and separation, which in all the planets (with the exception of the Moon) is [a time] of several days, pertains to the actual motion of seeking, which ceases, when those causes have ceased and their strength has elapsed, during the time while they were in force the native is seeking—if he wants to, and when he wants to. But when it has left off, he has no further interest in seeking or purchasing a dignity. And the same is the cause of motion toward revenge, extravagance, robbery, murder, etc.

But in the case of questions, the matter is quite otherwise. For if the *Caelum* contains the truth of a question only at that moment in which the question is made, which is arbitrary, it cannot have it any other way than from [the native's] will. And if it contains that at any particular moment, then any celestial figure will also contain that truth, and other absurd things will follow, which was said above and will be said [again] below.

Chapter 4. *The Doctrine of the Arabs Depends upon many Vain Assumptions.*

Strangely, the Arabs, the Indians, and the other Oriental Peoples take great care, and all the rest of those who follow them, so that they might persuade [everyone] that their own art of Interrogations is true. And if their responses do not succeed, they have many pretexts of excuses by which they console their own honor.

For they say *firstly* that someone is not capable of forming or proposing the question. Moreover, Hermes says in Aphorism 16,[1] *You should not define anything before you know the intention of the querent. Many people indeed do not know how to ask, and they cannot express what they have in mind.*

But truly, this escape is of no moment, since it is sufficient for the Astrologer, that he conceives the intention of the Querent, and he is able to reshape that question by saying, "Alas, he is foolish who comes to me questioning and does not know how to ask whether it is this or that that he wants to ask me about?" But if perchance the Astrologer were to speak, and the entire intent would be only in hearing, then the celestial influx would be changed or distorted, and that sought after truth would vanish, which would nevertheless be a foolishness to be feared.

They say *secondly* that there should be no response to a question proposed by way of testing or deriding. But how could the Astrologer know whether the Querent only intends to test or deride? Haly, Part. 1, Chapter 11, teaches how the Querent's thought may be found according to [the method of] Alkindi[2] and according to himself. For Alkindi, a celebrated Professor of this foolishness [says]:

> " That if you want to know the thought of the Querent, count the degrees that are from the ruler of the [planetary] hour up to the degree of the Sun, and cast what results from the beginning of Aries, and in the house where the number leaves off, there will be the thought; which you will judge by its own signs according to the nature of its ruler."

---

[1] A *Centiloquium* is attributed to Hermes in the medieval MSS. It is probably a medieval composition, but its author is unknown. There is an English translation by Henry Coley in his *Clavis Astrologiae Elimata* (London: Tooke & Sawbridge, 1676), Chapter XXI. "*Hermes Trismegistus,* his *Centiloquium* in *English*," pp. 329-339. See now my book *Five Medieval Astrologers* (Tempe, Az.: A.F.A., Inc., 2008), which contains a new translation of that *Centiloquy.*

[2] Probably the reference is to al-Kindî, *De iudiciis astrorum* 'The Judgments of the Stars' (Venice: Peter Liechtenstein, 1509). He is also cited in *The Book of Nine Judges.*

But truly, because the ruler of the [planetary] hour is [itself] merely fictitious, as we shall show below, this method of detecting the Querent's thought collapses. But Haly himself is little content with so brief a secret, and along with the other Arabs, he will have it that the significators of the thought are in the ninth from the ASC and the third from the ASC:

> "Those that are in the ASC (he says) are called ruler of the house, ruler of the exaltation, ruler of the terms, ruler of the face, ruler of the novena. Their own Almuten, the planet toward which the ASC degree is moving, and the planet that is found in the ASC. But those that are beyond the ASC are the Part of Fortune and its ruler, the ruler of the [planetary] hour and the ruler of the Sun by day or of the Moon by night. Consider, therefore (he says) which one of all these has more and stronger dignities and more rulership in the figure, because that one will be the significator of the thought."

Truly, Haly does something else by multiplying the fictitious rulers, especially those of the terms, the face, the novena, the hour (which are mere nonsense, as we have taught elsewhere), by which the mind of the Astrologer can conjecture in greater ignorance of the Querent's thought. Besides, Haly did not teach how the significator of the Querent's thought is to be used, so that this can become known. Indeed, because he himself didn't know how to use it, or (what is more probable) he had discovered that it does not correspond to experience. Whence, it is no wonder that the Chaldeans or the Babylonian Astrologers would not dare to say to King Nebuchadnezzar what they had thought about his dream, and only by a divine revelation was that judgment made to Daniel, who asserted to the King that the Magi and the Babylonian wise men could not judge that.

Then if someone, in order to put the science of astrology to the test, should ask whether his own brother is alive, whom he knows to be dead, knowledge which he has of the truth, doesn't it disturb the face of the *Caelum* that it does not signify that truth, or the mind of the Astrologer that he does not recognize it? That certainly cannot be said, just as neither the same thing is caused by the will of the Querent, for proving the science of astrology;. But it should rather be said that astrologers of that ilk are already rejecting the science for no other cause that it seeks, than because they are unable to deceive it. But they are able to beguile something unknown & credulous; and they therefore want this to be a property of their own science, that it is only proper to give true responses about things that are unknown to the Querent, but not about things that are already known.

But if they say that questions that are propounded for the sake of testing are not caused by the stars, but solely by the will of man, then consequently no reply should be given except to serious questions, or to someone who with the greatest care and anxiety for himself, or for another person about whom he is much concerned; comes by himself or [send his message] by another messenger, as Messahala[1] says in *The Book of the Nine Judges* "*namely, that he will have it that such questions are only impelled by the stars.*" Nevertheless, they cannot escape in that way, seeing that by knowing the truth of the question propounded he can propose it to the astrologer with serious and great care and anxiety for himself or for another, so that he may prove whether they are able to consider in other things that are also of great moment, because surely it is [a matter] of no little interest to that Querent and especially to Magnates.

To these things, add from Chapter 3 that they want the beginnings of all things to be like the birth of a man, and consequently to be caused by the *Caelum*; given which (but not conceded), they are required to respond to any question from their own principles, especially since there is no question for which some true response might not be suitable, either affirmative or negative: according to these axioms, *whatever is or is not, and concerning whatever,*

---

[1] The famous Mashâʾâllâh (d.c. 815).

there is a true affirmation or negation. From every side, therefore, it is plain how frivolous this second means of escape is.

Messahalla along with others says **third**. The question ought to be simple, and it is not proper to add another question to it, and everyone strongly commends this [rule]. And besides that, they do not want a question about the same thing to be made to two [different] astrologers, neither at the same time, nor in succession, nor twice to one of them. Which precaution is surely the principle one of all those for concealing the worthlessness of their own art. For from the responses of two or more astrologers on the same question, either at the same time or successively, it would be too evident that there would be as many main points as there are opinions—but no science—since science as a whole is uniform and certain with regard to its conclusions about the same thing if however it depends upon principles that are certain.

For the **third**, it is proved that this evasion is the most worthless. At whatever moment of time a question about any matter can be propounded to an astrologer, who will give a response for the truth to that same question. Therefore, if a question about that same matter is propounded to two astrologers, either at the same time or in succession, or to both of them together, nothing prevents their true responses from always being given regarding the truth of that question. The preceding is proved, then from the practice of these astrologers, who do not dismiss any Querent, whatever he seriously inquires about, by saying that at such a moment, there cannot be a response to such a question: but for any Querent they erect a figure and respond, unless one of them who is very scrupulous sees that the 7th house and its ruler are badly afflicted, in which case the astrologer sees that he is likely to give a false response, as Pontanus[1] explains in Aphorism 14 of his *Centiloquium*, which has this: *"in how many errors is the astrologer involved, when the seventh house and its ruler will be afflicted."*

---

[1] Giovanni Gioviano Pontano (1426-1503), *Centiloquium* (Venice, 1503).

And therefore he is afraid to respond, lest in his own foolish art he might make too obvious an error and then be criticized. Then, because children, when they are men, are not compelled by the stars to propound a question, but they may either delay it at their pleasure or propose it. Thence it follows that they can propound a question at any moment, and it is not possible to show an impossibility, either by one or by many Querents. The consequences are proved. For if at any moment in which any sort of question is propounded—at least, a serious one—they erect the figure and respond; and they suppose that at any moment the Caelum is disposed to giving responses to any sort of question.

Therefore, if a question is proposed about the same thing to two astrologers, either together, or in succession, or twice to one of them, there is nothing to prevent responses to be given always with regard to the truth of that question. But from that doctrine, what absurdities follow is stated in the following chapter. But this follows immediately, that if the question propounded is not a single one, as Messahala and the other will have it, but it has another different question adjoined to it, but from that same figure a response can be made to both. Add to these what Dorotheus [says] in Haly, Part 1, Chapter 11, contrary to Messahala:

> "If when you have many questions" (which understand to be at the same time from the same Querent), "take the first from the ASC, the 2nd from the MC, the 3rd from the 11th house, the 4th from the 5th, the 5th from the 7th, the 6th & 7th from the IMC, and the 8th from the 9th house." But others say "you will take the first question from the ASC, the 2nd from the second house, the 3rd from the third, and so on." Still others, "take the first question from the first application that the Moon has, the second from the second, and so on." Finally, others assert the succession: "if you take the first question from the ruler of the first hour, the second from the ruler of the second hour, etc., and so on successively down to the end of a few questions or of many; for you

ought to inquire" says Haly "and take note if, with God as a guide, you want to find [the ruler]."

But I say that it is absurd to think that God Himself will offer a guide to an astrologer running through these 4 different modes that are indeed incongruous and alien to a natural foundation, so that rather by prophesying than by studying them diligently, the truth of any question can be enunciated; and I marvel that those with the name of astrologer have not been ashamed to have expounded so much nonsense to wiser intellects. And so it remains to state how vain and indeed ridiculous the aforesaid precautions or evasions of the Arabs are, by which they try to defend their own art of questions.

Chapter 5. *The Doctrine of the Arabs on Interrogations is plainly False.*

Although from the fundamentals of this doctrine set forth above it is plain that it is false, yet lest there remain any doubt about that matter, the same things must be confirmed by an astrological demonstration thus.

A chart erected at the hour of a question according to the Arabs is of no truth per se with regard to the thing about which the query is made. Therefore, the doctrine of the Arabs about interrogations is plainly false. The preceding is proved, for when anyone queries an Astrologer for himself whether he will have wealth or dignities which the natal figure denies to him, certainly in whatever way the figure of the question is signifying such things, it will be foolish to suppose anything by that figure, or else the particular constitution of the *Caelum*—the character of the *Caelum*—impressed on the nativity and denying wealth or dignities would be destroyed, and a new impression would be made on the Querent, which would dispose him to wealth or dignities.

Otherwise no faith can be had in natal figures. For these two—the native will never have wealth (as is testified by the figure of the nativity), and someday he will have wealth (as is testified by the figure of the question)—are contradictory, which, if this one is true, then that one is false. But by the common consent of all Astrologers, also the Arabs themselves, the greatest and principal faith must be had in natal figures per se; therefore, no faith can be had in the figures of questions per se; and consequently, a chart erected at the hour of a question in the manner of the Arabs is per se of no truth, whence it is plain that the consequence is true, and vice versa, that if the nativity signifies wealth for the native, and especially strongly, it will be absurd to assert from the figure of a question that he will not have it.

The same thing must be said about someone querying for another person. Moreover, this demonstration is confirmed. For during the life of the native a thousand questions can be made, either by him, or by others, whether he is going to be rich from Chapter 4, and if the same question is proposed to many Astrologers, either at the same time, or successively, none of them asks the Querent whether the same question has already been proposed before, but immediately he will erect the figure and give a response.

None of the Arabs, moreover, asserts that so many different figures, are conformable to the radical figure and to each other with regard to the signification of wealth, when indeed they do not want the same question to be proposed twice by the same man, for fear of a diversity of figures, and from that a contrariety of judgment. And therefore, when from those same figures some of them signifying wealth, but others not, it can certainly be said that looked at in themselves they signify wealth or poverty, indeed they signify the same things or they forecast them, then to those who are being born in the places of those same figures, who are subject to those same figures, on which they depend, so that the effect comes from its own cause. But with respect to the Querent, who from these figures neither depends on being nor on interrogating, since his interrogation depends upon his will, unless by chance and by accident they can exhibit a true response—namely, on the hypothesis that a figure occurs that is similar to the radical in the signification of wealth.

But what if there are taken neither a thousand questions, nor even two, but once only there is proposed a legitimate question about the same thing, at that moment namely in which the Querent first asks, impelled by the *Caelum*, because then it contains in its signification the truth of the question.

I reply **first**, that this indeed is said by others, but not proved by them. I reply **second**, that impulse and signification of the *Caelum* at the moment of the interrogation have already been rejected above. I reply **finally**, the Querent asking for another whether he is going to marry a wife, can in no way hinder this, and not in his own case can he himself ask the same thing, since that thing pertains more to this person than to that one; for they offer a reason or a contrary procedure, namely one by which they ask from the Querent, whether he is the first or the only one who has made this interrogation? To which question very often and almost always the Querent will answer that he doesn't know; nevertheless, the Arab bears the opinion of the prophet.

For Hermes, Aphorism 98, says that the Moon in the 4th, 7th, 9th, or 12th *indicates that that cause has already been asked*,[1] and it indicates the same thing if it is separated from Mercury; and it can be confirmed neither by reason nor by experience, and it is not approved by any Arab.

The falsity of this same doctrine is proved thus **secondly**. since from Chapter 2 [we have said that] the Arabs suppose, or from their doctrine and practice it is deduced that they suppose, that at any moment the *Caelum* is disposed to giving responses on whatever is asked; therefore, whatever the present status of the *Caelum*, it contains the true responses to all questions that can be made about any kind of subject, whether it is present or past or future; and therefore, from the figure of the nativity of any man, or even of

---

[1] Aph. 98. "The Moon in the 4th, 7th, 9th, or 12th house shows the true cause of the question that has been propounded: the same thing is shown by her separation from Mercury. And if the Ascendant and the Moon are in double-bodied signs, the cause of the question is confirmed."

a dog, or whatever kind of figure of the question, everything can be said that to individual men, or animals, or plants, or artifacts about which a question can be made, has happened, is happening, or will happen; which silliness everyone cannot [fail to] see. Indeed, it would follow that all celestial figures are of the same signification,[1] and not anything is signified by one that is not signified by some other one, by which nothing can be thought to be more alien and insane from astrological knowledge.

It is proved **thirdly** from their practice. For if it is sought from an Arab, whether someone has married, or is now marrying, or is going to marry; he only perceives whether the figure signifies matrimony, so that he can respond about any time, past, present, or future; for he does not have legitimate considerations by means of which he can discern these [different] times. For if perchance he wants to say of the rulers of the signification in the angles, they signify present time; in succedents, future time; in cadents, past time; or in the case of their conjunction or aspect, partile signifies the present; application, the future; and separation, the past.

From that it could be concluded, in the figures of nativities, that the native has married and has held dignities before he was born, and he has no [such] disposition while he is being born, which things are declared to be ridiculous. Therefore, if the question is about the past, he will reply that he has married; if it is about the present, that he is marrying; and if about the future, that he will marry; namely, because the figure signifies marriage.

Indeed, if three persons were at the same time asking about marriage, one about the past, another about the present, and another about the future, the Arab, from the same figure, will reply to each

---

[1] This not true! Each question that is asked has its own set of significators in the chart. For example, one question might be about money, so the 2nd house and its ruler and planets in that house would be significators. While at the same time someone might ask a question about marriage, which would require an investigation of the 7th house, etc. So, as many as 12 different questions might be asked simultaneously that could be investigated by the same chart with different results in each case.

of them in the same way. Why not if 1,000 all together were asking, either for themselves, or for another, about matrimony, contracted in the past, the present, or the future. But he would reply, not affirmative to some of them, but negative to others, but affirmative to all or negative to all from the same figure, also contrary to the celestial decree of the nativity. The same thing will have to be said about any other sort of thing asked about at the same moment of time.

These things, moreover, are very absurd and alien to the manner of action of the stars; then, since the true principles of astrology have been set forth by us, there is no need here to show [it] more fully, since the doctrine of nativities given by us has proved that celestial figures are not significators, but rather they are effectors; or they are not signs, but rather they are causes. But that the same cause [acting] in so many men from their own natal figures that are very different, indeed having been contrarily disposed, could produce the same effect simultaneously, is utterly alien to the nature of causes; for the agent follows the disposition of the patient, and whatever is received is received according to the nature of the patient, as is known to philosophers; consequently, the Sun's heat at the same time hardens mud and melts wax.[1]

It is proved **fourthly** from their manner of predicting. For they do not even agree among themselves on the first principles of making a judgment; and however much they do agree would be an absurd agreement, just like their mode of making a judgment. First of all, it is plain that all of them allot the first house of the figure to the Querent; and yet about the house for the astrologer (whom they make to be the judge of the question), they quarrel among themselves, and not yet have they been able to ascertain for themselves a definite house [for the astrologer]; and that is as it should be,

---

[1] A favorite saying of Morin. I don't know its origin. An early citation is found in the *Book Explaining the Elemental Figures of the Demonstrative Art* by Ramón Lull (c.1235-c.1315), which was written around 1283. In astrology, it means that the nature and status of the person receiving a particular influx from the *Caelum* will affect the result that the influx has on him. Ptolemy points this out in the early chapters of *Tetrabiblos*, Book 1.

since they are only false judges, trying to persuade themselves in that moment when they erect the figures of the questions, that they are inspired by heaven, like those who once upon a time gave oracles from a tripod,[1] when nevertheless the *Caelum* does not breathe inspiration into them with regard to a propounded question, as was said in Chapter 3.

Many astrologers agree on the 10th house, which is [the house] of dignity and honor. Moreover, an astrologer is a judge worthy of honor. Others cast him down from the tenth to the seventh, since they say that that is more fitting for him, as Pontano will have it in his *Commentary* on the 14th aphorism of the *Centiloquy*.[2] Its reason is that the first house is commonly given to the Querent; moreover, he comes to the astrologer as being ignorant of the thing that he wants to know. Ignorance, moreover, and knowledge are diametrically opposed; therefore, if the first [house] is destined for the Querent, the seventh, diametrically opposed to the first, is destined for the astrologer.

And therefore Ptolemy says in that Aphorism, *In so many errors the astrologer is involved, when the seventh house and its ruler will be afflicted.*[3] Namely, because if malefics were in the seventh or rule it when badly afflicted, some misfortune will happen to the astrologer (as they will have it) because they cannot think otherwise than that he will pronounce something false for the truth. Truly, the tenth house is only [the house] of actions and dignities of the native himself, or in the sense of the vigor of the thing to which the first house is attributed, but the seventh is [the house] of the spouse or the enemies of the native, or in the sense of the decline of the thing to which the first house is attributed, as we have said elsewhere.

---

[1] A reference to the famous Oracle at Delphi in Greece.
[2] I do not have Pontano's *Commentary*, but the text of the Aphorism is given below.
[3] Actually, it reads (as translated from the Greek version), "Oh, how many things baffle the learned one, when the 7th house and its ruler are afflicted." But the Latin versions substitute *astrologer* for *learned one*.

But these are plainly alien to the judge of the question. I, therefore, am surprised that they have not rather given the fourth to the astrologer, which is [the house] of secret things to be revealed by him, or to the ninth, which is [the house] of sciences and prophecies, or at least to the first, because when the question has been proposed he begins to be the judge, and then the tenth could be given to his action, which is to judge, or to his dignity; but the seventh could be given to the querent or to his question, like a lawsuit that is terminated by a judge, and this conception would be more reasonable than the previously mentioned doctrine of the Arabs.

Whatever is done, I would counsel the judge that if in his figure of the houses one of them is not pleasing to him on account of its misfortune that he betake himself to another more fortunate, and from there, free from malefics, he bring forth his opinion, since the sum of the whole matter consists of this—that the astrologer responds truthfully, and the Aphorism can be applied to any house which is assigned to the astrologer, to whom, nevertheless, from what was said above no [house] should be assigned.

But we should let all agree on two determined houses—one for the Querent, and another for the astrologer; and we may see how absurd the agreement is. In whatever kind of question that is propounded, four things occur—the person making the query, the question itself, the thing that is quesited, and the judge or astrologer. The first house of the figure is given to the Querent, since he is making the query, the tenth or the seventh to the astrologer. The thing that is quesited belongs to the house which has its essential signification, as if the question is about friends, it belongs to the eleventh, about a wife to the seventh, about dignities to the tenth; which, understand that from their mind [these are] the houses of the figure of the question, but not of the figure of the nativity of him for whom the question is made—to which figure they pay no notice—and very often they do not have it.[1]

---

[1] Since in the old times most people did not know their birth time (or often even their birth date), the only thing an astrologer could do to answer a question would be to erect a Horary chart. This is why Horary astrology was so prevalent.

Moreover, they assign no house to the question, although it should nevertheless belong to the first, since that question begins to exist, which previously did not, and so the house of the Querent and the question will be the same. But already the celestial constitution makes its influx into none of those four at the moment of the question, since it is supposed that those are related to the question according to Chapter 3. And so it does nothing with regard to any of them, since it cannot act without an influx. And consequently it has no signification with regard to any of them, since it does not signify any thing that it does not do. Where then will the whole question depart from? Or from whence will its true response come forth? Let them answer this question with a true response if they are able.

Besides the significations of the houses, which in Chapter 3 we reported from Haly, ought to agree with the thing to which the first house is attributed, for it is plain from the doctrine of nativities that the first house is of course that of the man who is being born, the second of his wealth, the third of his brothers, and so on with the others. But already in this doctrine of questions the first house is attributed to the Querent or to the question; therefore the second house according to Haly will be the significator of the worth of the Querent or of the question; the third of that which happens to the Querent or the question, and that which is joined to it of the same sort; the fourth will signify the offspring of the Querent or of the question and their roots, and so on with the rest.

But these do not concern the thing which is quesited, nor should they refer to it, certainly because the first house is not attributed to that thing, which house is only that of beginning things, but the thing that is quesited, if it is [something that] is going to be, has not yet begun to be, as if it is quesited about a future marriage, or about a future dignity. Perchance they would say that the Querent asking for himself about that is the thing itself about which it is being quesited, whether it is for example that he is going to marry, or that he is going to acquire a dignity; and at the moment that he asks the question, then he begins to be the Querent, which before that he was not.

But except that in this case the appellations of the houses of the natal figure ought to be retained, and moreover not altered, as Haly did: when the Querent does not ask for himself but for another person, as if he asks whether his brother may be alive, who is nevertheless dead and has ceased to be; or if he asks about any other kinds of things not pertaining to himself, which are either no more, or are in the future, but at least they have not already begun to be, the futility of a superior evasion is detected, and all the more because when he only asks this about his brother—whether he is alive or dead—what conformity have the significations of the houses with this particular question? If you exempt the third house, which is said to be [the house] of brothers? Should the significations of the other houses necessarily be examined, as whether this is [the house of] the brother, or whether he was or will be rich, whether he may marry or has married or is going to marry, etc.? Before it is determined that the brother is alive or dead, because a single response is expected, with the other things not even acknowledged.

But let us see at last how they might judge on illness, or the illness of the brother of him who asks. Since the question is about brothers, they consider the third house of the figure, which is [the house] of brothers; and if they see malefics in the third or ruling the third, or the ruler of the twelfth in the third, or the ruler of the third in the twelfth or conjunct the ruler of the twelfth, the Arabs judge the brother of the Querent to be ill. But the question is [really] about death, and not merely about illness; if, therefore, they see the third badly afflicted by malefics, or the ruler of the third, especially if a malefic is in the eighth, or its malefic ruler is in the third. Or the ruler of the third conjunct, square, or opposite the ruler of the eighth, especially [if it is] a malefic badly afflicted, they assert that the Querent's brother is dead; and by the same kind of reasoning, they judge all other questions of the twelve houses.

But I ask the Arab whether the twelfth house and the eighth of the figure of the question are the houses of the illnesses and death of the Querent or whether [they are those] of the brother about whom he asks[1]? It cannot be said that they are those of the Querent; otherwise, there cannot be concluded from them the illness or the death of the brother, but rather of the Querent [himself]; nor can it also be said that they are [the houses] of the illnesses and death of the brother himself, for since the twelfth and the eight are such [only] with respect to the first [house], which is given to the Querent, not to the brother, they will [only] be the houses of illnesses and death with respect to the Querent, but not to the brother, to whom is given the third [house]. Let them, therefore, resolve this argument if they are able. For I do not see how they can resolve it. For these things, brothers, parents, the wife, and children depend less for their own accidents on the natal figure of the native, than on their own nativity. For on the former they depend only generally, although it is a natural figure; but they depend particularly on their own nativity. How much less, therefore, do they depend on the figure of a question, which is not even natural, but only arbitrary?

Whence, it is plain that the whole doctrine of questions of the Arabs has no natural foundation but only an arbitrary one. Finally, every celestial figure ought to be the cause of those things that it signifies; and that is plain in figures, either in universal constitutions, or in the particular figures of nativities; otherwise the stars would have no active powers; but the Arabian figures of questions are not causes, but only signs of those things that they signify, [based] on the hypothesis that they signify those things. For when it is asked whether someone is alive or dead, a pauper or rich, etc., the figure erected for the question confers nothing effectively about his death, his life, his wealth, his poverty, etc., which often are [things that existed] a long time before that figure; therefore, the erection of that figure and the judgment following from it are

---

[1] Here Morin points out the difference between what might be called the "universal meaning" of houses and their "derived" meaning. The use of derived houses goes back to the Classical Period. They are mentioned by Vettius Valens, *Anthology*, ix. 3. 6. See my book, *A History of Horoscopic Astrology* (Tempe, Az.: A.F.A., Inc., 1996), pp. 55-56; 2nd ed. (2006), pp. 57-58, for an example.

mere stupidities, lacking any natural foundation; and this reasoning is very true.

From the above said reasons, it is therefore sufficient, and more so most evident that the whole doctrine of the Arabs on questions is plainly false, which we had undertaken to show.

Chapter 6. *The Doctrine of the Arabs on Questions is Fraudulent.*

That doctrine can be proven to be fraudulent in many ways.

First. Because, since Chapter 5 has shown it to be false, it necessarily follows that it is fraudulent. Therefore, [so are] all those who consult it about any thing whatever.

Second. Because if at any moment it can respond to any sort of question, the Arabs are deceived by their own precautions, saying that two astrologers, either at the same time or successively cannot render a true opinion about the same question. But if a response cannot be rendered, then the Arabs are wrong, when at whatever moment a question is proposed to them they erect a figure and respond from it. For first it must be considered whether that moment is appropriate for a true response. And if it is not, the questioning should be set aside, which, nevertheless, they do not do, let they lose the profit offered to them; for they are more concerned with profit than with truth or fame; for when they are apprehended to be liars, they have their own precautions and false refuges, which they set before the deceived Querents for the protection of their own doctrine and fame.

Third. Because in order to embellish their entirely false art with some pretense, they also use in their practice selected aphorisms of true astrology or of the doctrine of nativities, which they apply to their own figures. Since, however, there is a great disparity between the figures of nativities, which are natural, and the figures of questions, which are only arbitrary, depending on no true foundation, [their action is] plainly similar to [that of] superstitious geomanticists, which to their own figures of merely fortuitous points (unless they occur by the will of the Master Devil, the ruler of the hands of the Geomanticist, who is not obliged to pay attention to the number of points that he notes in his chart; and consequently, their number is merely fortuitous, or it is at the will of the Devil) they falsely attribute the signs and the planets, and the strengths of these, so that before the inexperienced they set off the art of their superstition to advantage, and they conceal its diabolical falsity.

Chapter 7. *The Doctrine of the Arabs on Interrogations is Diabolical.*

It is proved first because from Chapter 5 it is false, and from Chapter 6 it is fraudulent. Moreover, the Devil was the first liar and deceiver; consequently, he is the prime author of every falsity and fraud.

Second, because when the Arabs say that the Querent is compelled by the stars at the moment of the question or of access to an astrologer, they overturn the freedom of choice of the Querent and they introduce fatal necessity; and they cannot induce it from the principles of their own art because it is heretical, contrary to the true religion, and consequently diabolical. Whence, it is no wonder that the Turks, Arabs, and all the other Mohammedans and Oriental Pagans are alien to the true religion, so firmly do they believe in the fatal necessity [produced] by the stars, and on account of that doctrine of the Arabs, astrological science was almost always condemned by the Roman Popes.

Third, because the Devil introduced it into the true astrology, so that he might defame and deprave it, lest men acknowledge the proper and genuine powers of the stars, and then return due praises to God, but rather that they might be blinded, but blinded, so that they might be converted to [belief in] the figments of terms, faces, novenas, decans, pitted degrees, light degrees, smoky degrees, etc.[1] And so they are deceived, and they deceive others, not only in regard to astrological responses, but also in regard to works of Magic, towards which the Devil also distorted and propagated superstition from the stars.

Chapter 8. *The Falsity of Responses to Interrogations from the Ruler of the Planetary Hour.*

The Arabs, in their own doctrine of interrogations attribute much virtue to the rulers of the planetary hours.[2] No one should marvel at how varied and vain those same Arabs, Chaldeans, Egyptians, and Indians make games with the seven-fold number of the planets with regard to the years of the native, by Alfridaries,[3] and with regard to single days through the planetary hours. For, seduced by the Devil by means of these, they have converted those offering worship to the true God to idolatry; also, in the natural sciences, and especially in astrology the most divine of all of them, instead of truth they have chosen to graze on fictions. Among which, the doctrine they have handed down about planetary hours, or with the planet said to be ruling[4] a particular hour of the day (which some call the ruler of the cycle), claims not the least place for itself. But all should marvel that at this time also no few astrologers, nor

---

[1]In the earlier books of the *Astrologia Gallica*, Morin stated his belief that those subdivisions of the zodiac were entirely valueless. His main reason was that (at least in his opinion) they had no relation to astronomy, but were entirely arbitrary.

[2]The Arabs learned about planetary hours from Greek astrology books that they had translated into Arabic. It was the Greek-speaking astrologers of Alexandria who invented the planetary hours and named the days of the week after the planets. The fourth century astrologer Paul of Alexandria, *Introduction to Astrology*, explains the whole thing in Chapters 20 & 21. But Morin did not know this, and he supposed that planetary hours were a wicked Arabian invention.

[3]Alfridaries (their name is derived from the Persian *fardar* 'time period') are profections using arbitrarily defined time-periods that are said to be ruled by the planets. They were commonly used by the Greek astrologers, and after them by the Persian and Arabian astrologers. The Hindu astrologers also make much use of an elaborate group of them. But even Ptolemy has a simple scheme of them, since he assigns various years of a person's life to the planets.

[4]Reading *dominante* 'dominating' instead of *dimanante* 'spreading abroad'.

those of little reputation among Christians, mention that falsehood for a great secret; and those also especially rely upon [them] for predicting the accidents of the individual hours of any particular day from the present state of the ruler of whichever planetary hour.

Since, moreover, that doctrine is entirely false, and, unless I am mistaken, introduced by the Devil along with the other figments of the Arabs, it seems good to show its falsity here, lest with regard to it minds should any longer be seduced.

First, therefore, they make both the artificial day and the artificial night to be divided into twelve hours, which they call planetary; and most of them make these equal by dividing the arc of the equator that ascends by day into twelve equal parts for the twelve diurnal hours, and the one that ascends by night similarly into twelve equal parts for the twelve nocturnal hours. But many make these unequal, having divided the mean of the zodiac ascending by day or by night into twelve equal parts, whose ascensions will be unequal both by day and by night.

With regard to which supposition, I say first, the division of the day and night into twenty-four hours is not natural, but arbitrary, as is the division of the hour into 60 minutes; consequently, there cannot be any natural foundation for any planetary virtue; and this reason is a very strong one.

Second, it must previously be agreed whether in truth the ecliptic ought to be divided, and a valid natural scheme for one division rather than another offered, which nevertheless is offered by no astrologer that I have seen.

Third, that division of the artificial day and night cannot be made in the arctic regions turned towards the poles of the world, where the Sun does not rise and set during 24 hours; but the day, or the not artificial day lasts many days, or even natural months. Consequently, the doctrine of planetary hours is not scientific, since it is not universal, but only particular.

Second. They propose to assign individual planets to individual hours for rulers of those hours, having taken the origin from the rising of the Sun; and that planet from which the day has its name, with the other planets in their own order and circularly distributed through the individual 24 hours; for example, if it is the day of Jupiter, which is named after Jupiter, Jupiter will rule in that day the first hour of that day from the rising of the Sun, Mars will preside over the second, the Sun over the third, and so on, up to the 24 hours of the day and night. By which order, Venus will be found to rule the first hour of the day of Venus named after it. And because the same thing follows in the individual days, these astrologers think some great and divine mystery exists in this, by which the individual planets are truly made powerful in succession for ruling the individual hours.

But this game is very nicely shown in the following figure [see page 35], in which the circumference of the circle is divided into 7 equal parts; and having put Saturn in one point of the division, the other planets, that is Jupiter, Mars, Sun, Venus, Mercury, and the Moon, successively to the left in accordance with its order, in the other points; from any planet to those second removed are drawn lines, which form 7 isosceles triangles. and there is the mystery: from the planet Saturn, which is called the Saturn-day, by the Christians the Sabbath, and rules over its first hour, follow the line that leads to the left and it will indicate the Sun, which calls the following day Sun-day, by the Christians Dominican, and it rules the first hour of it. Another line drawn from the Sun indicates the Moon, which gives its name to the following day Moon-day, and it rules the first hour of it. another line that is drawn from the Moon indicates Mars, which gives its name to the following day Mars-day, and it rules the first hour after sunrise of it, and so with the rest according to the order of the days.

If, moreover, the first hour of the day of the Sabbath is given Saturn for its ruler, the second Jupiter, the third Mars, etc. in sequence according to their own order, or if the one that those planets have in the Ether descending from the *Caelum* to the Earth, up to 24 hours; it will happen that the Sun will in order be the ruler of the first hour of Sun-day, or Dominican, and so with the others. Which—and certainly a mystery if it contained the truth attributed to it by the Arabs—cannot be accommodated by the Copernican Hypothesis, which indeed does not admit such an order of the planets.[1]

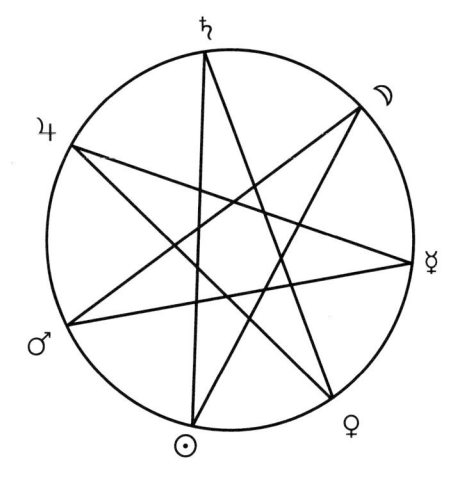

But these three assumptions about the individual planets assigned to the individual hours, having taken the beginning from the rising of the Sun rather than from its setting, or noon, or midnight, and from the planet for which the day is named, are mere fictions without any logic—that things have themselves thus—and so it should not be done otherwise, and without constant experience which the promoters of this doctrine can offer, even though they propose something fortuitous. But what consists of a mystery in this, as with the hours of each day distributed thus to the individual planets, is that it always happens that the planet that is ruler of the first hour of any day would be the one giving its name to that same day.

---

[1] Here Morin challenges the order of the planets: Saturn, Jupiter, Mars, Sun, Venus, Mercury, Moon, and says that it is wrong. But he thereby contradicts himself because he accepts the traditional rulership of the signs by the planets, which is established based on exactly that same order. And it is Greek, rather than Arabic.

I say **first**. That would also be done if the first hour were taken from noon, as is more pleasing to some, or even any other hour; consequently, for the naming of the day, it doesn't matter which planet rules any particular hour of the day, namely because any hour of the day can be attributed to the planet that gives its name to the day.

I say **second**. From this, therefore, it is plain that the naming of the days is less important than the above said distribution of the planets through the individual hours, and the naming of those days was taken from the planets ruling the first or whatever hour of the day thus occurring. Which is proved from this, because the order of the days has no conformity with the natural order of the planets, yet the order of the hours still observes it.[1]

I say **third**. That even if the rulership of the planets over the individual hours of the day from the rising of the Sun or from noon would be natural and not fictitious, yet nothing would concern how any particular day was named, since the planet that rules the hour receives no virtue from that naming. Which reason is stronger from this, because the usual beginning of the day to which that naming pertains is diverse among various nations. For the old Egyptians began their day at the middle of the night, and they ended it at the middle of the following night,[2] which custom the Gauls, the Spanish, the Germans, and many other nations follow, along with the Roman Church. The Babylonians began the day with the rising of the Sun[3]; the Jews, and now the Italians, from the setting of the Sun, and so with the other nations.

---

[1] Not so! The order of the planetary hours is the so-called *heptaone*, Saturn, Jupiter, Mars, Sun, Venus, Mercury, and Moon. And this is a natural order of the planets because it lists them in the order of their observed motion in the Caelum, from slowest, Saturn, to the fastest, the Moon.

[2] This is wrong! The old Egyptians began the day at sunrise. It was the Romans who began it at midnight. The Catholic Church followed the Roman custom, so it eventually spread to most of Europe.

[3] Wrong again! Actually, the Babylonians began the day at sunset, so that night came first, followed by day, but the portion of the 24-hour period called "day" began at the following sunrise.

How, therefore, will this naming of the days be established with these diverse customs, even in the same Kingdom, since many [peoples] can be subjugated, and the mode of beginning the day so often changed? Finally, let the promoters of this foolishness explain, if they can, how and by which it is conferred on each planet three or four in a day, and the ruler ship of the hours is taken away, especially since Mercury, Venus, the Sun, and Mars, and particularly Jupiter and Saturn, in 7 hours vary their celestial state among themselves incessantly.

But from what was said above more sufficiently the foolishness and folly of those, who to resolve whatever question is offered, either something for himself, or for another, undertake to predict what is going to be at any particular hour of the day from the present celestial state of the ruler of the planetary hour. Add to this, that if anyone has asked at the first hour of the day, he will obtain one response from the ruler of that hour, if the interrogation is made at the second hour, he will obtain another and perhaps contrary response, and so on with the other hours; from which, the silliness of this doctrine is evident.

How greatly, moreover, important it is to overturn the universal doctrine of questions placed above and to exclude it from the science of true astrology, is well known from this [fact]—that it keeps its professors entangled in the obscurities of ignorance, it occupies them in [making] illegitimate profit from deceiving too credulous Querents; as many of those as those it delivers to the Devil, its author; and it defames the true science. Which evils in the world are not small, and not unfruitful of others; consequently, such astrologers ought to be punished.

Chapter 9. *Containing Cardan's Errors in his Short Treatise on Questions.*

Cardan, finally made wiser with regard to astrological questions, composed a short treatise on them,[1] in the preface of which he forewarns that even though he has often condemned other questions, he was still necessarily led to write about them, because many want to know a question (namely about the significators of the nativity), but not everything; and he says that this part [of astrology] is as equally natural and conjectural as the other one about nativities, to which he himself pays attention, at least for the most part. And in the truth of the matter, that doctrine of interrogations should only be admitted that is subordinated to the doctrine of nativities; and he resolved questions from the natal horoscope of the Querent or of him for whom the question [is propounded]. Nevertheless, Cardan committed errors about that doctrine that were not minor, some of which at least will be pointed out by us here, lest [those who are] too much devoted to Cardan may follow him further in this part [of astrology].

First, therefore, to the primary question. How much will the King conquer? He decided to judge according to the nativity of the King: and that was indeed correct. But he added "that if you do not have the nativity, you will find the moment in which he began to reign, for if he is a legitimate heir [to the throne], you will take the moment in which the previous King, either his father or his brother, died; but if it came about by election, the moment in which he was elected. And then you ought to erect the figure. And you will select, as in nativities, the aphetic place, and you will direct, and you will also make the progressions and the ingresses for the individual years."

In these also Cardan errs. For on whatever day or hour the King of France or Spain, etc. may die, in those places in which the Kingdom is hereditary, in whatever manner the *Caelum* is disposed at

---

[1] Jerome Cardan, *Opera omnia*, vol. 5, *De Interrogationibus Libellus*, pp. 553-560.

that moment, his legitimate successor is recognized as King by the law of the land, which has the procedure of the secondary fate, as Ptolemy says[1]: by the first and superior fate, that is by the celestial bodies, then by those not even supporting the new King, unless that happens by chance; indeed, not even in his own nativity by those things supporting a Kingdom for him, but rather by those denying it. Therefore, he has the Kingdom by the law of the land and not by the stars, unless the law were to be such that the son would not be King on the death of his father, as happens in Poland, Venice, and elsewhere, where the Kingdom is given to someone elected; and this is accustomed to be done in the German Empire. If, therefore, the succeeding son does not have the Kingdom from [the influence of] the stars, it is certainly absurd to erect a celestial figure for the moment when he succeeds, so that it may be known how many years the King is going to survive. For if that figure does not give the Kingdom, all the less will it give his duration in the Kingdom or the life of the King as King. Add [to that] that in the same way from a figure erected at the moment of the death of whoever's father, there would be a judgment on the length of life of his heir—indeed, of each individual heir—if there were more involved, as when it happens to rulers, who when dying divide their own Kingdoms among their children, who, from a figure erected at the moment of the death of their father, should all die on the same day; but these things are alien to reason and experience, and the practice of astrologers should not be concerned with these things.

But that which pertains to Kingdoms and to other dignities that are conferred by elections, although the hour of the election can be accelerated or retarded by the choice of the electors, and likewise the hour of the coronation of a King, which for that reason Cardan rejected as being not at all natural, but rather arbitrary: Nevertheless, it is certain that in the case of elections to dignities the celestial influxes assume for themselves no little jurisdiction. For no one is elected to honors and dignities, for whom the stars in his na-

---
[1]Ptolemy, *Tetrabiblos*, Book 1, Chapter 1.

tivity do not presage dignities, also at the very time of the election, by directions, revolutions, and transits; indeed, the figure erected at the moment of the election by its own influx supports the election, and in a way is similar in its signification to the radical influx, which reduces [it] from potential to an act. And from this a judgment can be made as to whether the election is fortunate or unfortunate, but all these influxes are only determined with respect to that dignity, but not to [the native's] life, in order to indicate its length. Which is more evidently plain from this, because for whatever dignity is conferred through election by a King, it would have to be judged as it would be for a Kingdom [obtained] by election. But the King can successively confer very many dignities on the same man [who is] dear to him or famous, the various figures of which would display a great confusion with regard to the term of life. Whence, I judge this method to be fallacious and alien to reason for [judging] the term of life of a King, or of any other person, who attains a dignity [either] by gift or by payment; and I judge that a true opinion [on this matter] can only be brought forth from the figure of the nativity. And yet I would not deny that from a figure erected at the moment of the election of a King, a Pope, a Chancellor, etc., it might be conjectured whether the elected person, having been granted or having purchased a dignity, will remain in it for a long time; but this conjecture will be a weak one unless it is confirmed by the natal figure.

For the second question, "What sort of administration will the King have?" Cardan wants to make the judgment not from the King's own nativity or some other one, but entirely from the beginning of his reign, that is from the moment in which he became the sovereign, as is plain from the fourth question, namely from a celestial figure erected at that moment.

But this doctrine is evidently false for this reason: because, aside from the fact that no one knows that beginning, it is contrary to the truth of the nativity, which is either null or else it must state what sort of administration the King will have, what will be his habits and his ability; and the natal influx of the *Caelum* with regard to his actions and dignities, to which are added the annual revolutions, and then the directions. Moreover, Cardan's rules with regard to this question are mere nonsense clashing with principle, which whoever wants to can see.

For the third question. "Whether Kings are friends?" He wants to conjecture this from their nativities and from the beginnings of their reigns; even if the closest places agree in principles, he pronounces the Kings to be friends to friendly Kingdoms. But if not, he judges either the Kings to be enemies and also their Kingdoms, or the King to be a friend and the Kingdom an enemy, or the other way around.

But if Cardan were alive, I would ask him whether he had ever known [the actual time of] the beginning of any Kingdom to be conformable to the figure erected [for it]? Or whether he had seen an astrologer among the ancients or the moderns who boasted of such knowledge? Or who at least had erected the figure of such a beginning? Nonsense! Therefore, from nativities alone must the question be resolved, since neither the Kingdom nor the State is a proper subject and per se the influx of the stars, which is only received from them by those things that are naturally generated, as has been set forth by us fully elsewhere.

For the fourth question. "Of Kingdoms warring mutually, which will be the winner?" says Cardan. "If you have the beginnings of the Kingdoms, that is best; and if you don't have them, you have the beginnings in which such Kings began to reign. In the third place, it is that you have the beginning of another deliberation of the waging their war. Fourth, if all of these are lacking, you have the nativities of those and of the leading generals. Finally, if you have none of these, you will take the testimony from Mars."

Moreover, it is plain that Cardan wants these five to succeed each other in the order of their power, and the figure of the nativity is therefore less certain than the three preceding it for solving the question, which nevertheless is the most false. For in the first place it is ignored by all, and even if it should be known, it is useless, as was made plain above. For the second, even if the King began to reign at that fortunate moment, yet if from his own nativity he is unfortunate in dignity, undertakings, and wars, he will certainly fail in the presence of another King with a nativity fortunate in those same things, especially if at the time of the conflict there is a fortunate direction and revolution. And to doubt this is to ignore the principles of astrology or to overturn its more certain doctrine, which is that of nativities. Moreover, of the third it cannot be known whether the moment of decision to wage war is lucky, or an unlucky one for the one making a decision, unless when his natal figure is compared, in which the Sun, or the Moon, or Jupiter himself, or Venus, or Mars, can be the significators of death, who would falsely trust the supporters of life in the figure of the deliberation.

Finally, the fifth is plainly absurd, since Mars in a very general signification does not signify anything in particular, as we have very often stated. And therefore the truth can only be given from the nativities of Kings and their generals, [but] not having rejected the figure of the decision for war, from which it can be seen whether the aggressor who decided to wage war decided to do so at a lucky or an unlucky moment; and usually too a figure that is erected for the conflict of Princes is valid, compared with the figures of the nativities. For it is certain that at that time in which great things, either good, or evil are done, the *Caelum* is disposed to them with respect to the particular men to whom they primarily and per se pertain.

For question Six. *Who will be the victor in a single combat?* He wants, if their nativities are not known (to which he has generally conceded the trustworthiness), a figure should be erected for the moment in which the firm and irrevocable decision was made, from which judgment is made, giving the first house to the aggressor, the seventh to his adversary, and the tenth to the judge.

Truly in the case of single combat there is the decision of the aggressor and the agreement of both [the participants], which is the principal and firm moment. For without the agreement of both, there will not be a single combat or a duel. Moreover, in the figure erected for this moment (common for both of the enemies), why will the first house be given to the aggressor rather than to his adversary? And when a duel takes place, an action belonging to the tenth house, why is it not given to the other one of the contenders, or divided between both of them, but [instead] is given to the judge, who does nothing in connection with that duel? Whether a judge is ignorant from [the nature of] his own nativity, stupid, or sycophantic, by the celestial state of the tenth house in the figures of the questions, he is made to be learned, wise, and fair,[1] since it cannot be said that in such figures the *Caelum* influences the astrologer against one rather than against the other, since the choice of an astrologer is free, and in the truth of the matter it influences against neither science nor wisdom; and no house can be assigned to the judge [as is stated] in Chapter 5.

From these things, therefore, the futility of such a doctrine is plain; and because an opinion must only be rendered from the figures of nativities, from the moment of the agreement to have a duel and from the hour of the conflict, as was said about [judgments involving] Kings. For these three contain the truth of the question. But these [remarks] concerning Cardan's error regarding questions is sufficient.

Chapter 10. *General Categories to which all Questions Propounded to Astrologers can be Reduced.*

Since we are only involved in the theory of Astrology here, therefore the doctrine of questions is only discussed by us here in general terms. We are going to treat of particular questions more fully in our *Astrological Practice* if God, the Best and Greatest, grants us life for it.[2]

---

[1] Not necessarily true! The condition of the 10th house would indicate the nature of the judge and the quality of his judgment.
[2] Which, alas, He did not. The reference is to another book that Morin had in mind

Moreover, we may call those questions legitimate that pertain either to constitutions naturally particular to natives, as to Peter[1] or to his horse, or to the universal constitutions of the planets, namely their revolutions, either periodic or synodic. But we judge all the rest to be illegitimate and incapable [of giving] a scientific response. As if it might be questioned how long this house will last, or this ship, or this state. Or what the appearance of a wolf signifies, or the conflict of a falcon and a kite seen in the air, or who has stolen his money from Peter, etc.

Furthermore, it seems to me that legitimate questions can generally be reduced to six categories: namely,

1. To accidents that are peculiar to the native in his life, his habits, his understanding, his wealth, his brothers, his parents, his children, etc. Namely, whether he is going to have brothers, a wife, etc. Whether he is going to love those persons. whether he is going to be happy with them, and such like [questions], in which only something is sought about the native in regard to those persons.

2. For accidents common to the native and those other persons such as agreement, disagreement, business dealings, lawsuits, duels, contracts with brothers, parents, children, his spouse, servants, bosses, friends, [and] enemies.

3. For the particular accidents of persons closely associated with the native, such as by what kind of death and when the father, the brother, the wife, the children will die: at what time a son is going to marry, whether a wife is chaste, etc.

4. For the accidents of persons not closely associated with the native by his own nativity, such as when the King is going to be victorious, or which of two warring Kings is going to be the victor.

---

to write covering the general practice of astrology.

[1] Morin uses the name 'Peter' as we would use 'Joe Doakes' to signify any particular person.

5. For general accidents depending upon a universal constitution,[1] such as war, plague, famine, floods, etc.

6. For general accidents not depending on a universal constitution, such as the King's administration, navigation, the beginning of commercial ventures by many associates.

Chapter 11. *How in general Questions belonging to those six Categories should be judged.*

No legitimate question should be judged only by a figure erected for the moment in which the question was propounded. For such a figure contains no truth unless by chance with regard to that question, as is sufficiently well-established by the preceding chapters. And this method was only invented, by the instigation of the Devil, by greedy and haughty idlers skilled to some extent in astrology, for the sake of profit and vain fame, namely so that among the ignorant they might boast that they could solve whatever sort of question is propounded, and they overlook no occasion for profit, but from the mad curiosity of wretched men they rake in the money from all sides; and in order that their ignorance and fraud not be detected, they cover them up with many vain precautions, as was made plain above. But the doctrine of judging every question is founded on celestial charts, either of nativities or of general constitutions.

And so [to consider] questions of the first kind about the personal and particular accidents of the native: it must only be answered from the figure of his nativity. As, if he asks whether he will acquire dignities, the 10th house, which is [the house] of dignities, must be inspected, and it must be seen what signs, planets, and fixed stars occupy it or rule it. Whether they are of a benefic or a malefic nature, then whether those planets are well or badly disposed by their celestial state, as well as how they are related to the

---

[1] The most common example of a 'universal constitution' is the Aries Ingress for a particular place.

ASC and its ruler, and to the Lights. Then, whether they are in good or bad houses of the figure, and, from a careful inspection of these, the response must be given, as will be taught in our *Astrological Practice*,[1] whose theory, however, is all contained in Book 21. and the same thing must be done in similar fashion for questions about wealth, brothers, children, the marriage partner, etc. whether the native will have such things and be fortunate in connection with them, according to Aphorism 17 of [the *Centiloquy*] of Hermes:

> "When you have been asked about the father, look at the fourth, about a brother the third, about a child the fifth, about a wife the seventh. But if you are asked about a sick person, you should interpret the ASC only."

But if the question is propounded for a fixed time, such as whether the native will marry in this month, the radical directions must be added, then the annual revolution and the monthly ones, and also their directions. Opinions must be taken from these; and the procedure is the same in other [questions].

For questions of the second kind, which are about accidents to the native in common with other persons, as a duel undertaken with an enemy, the nativities of both persons must be seen, their directions and revolutions at the time of the duel; indeed, a figure erected for the hour of the duel for which they have come together, and from all these considered in turn the response should be delivered. If it is asked about conjugal relations or agreement, let the nativities of the husband and the wife be seen,[2] not only whether they agree or disagree among themselves, or with the ASC, or the rulers of these are opposed to each other, or square, and these rulers are malefic by nature, but also whether from the husband's own figure

---

[1] Again, the book that Morin intended to write, but which unfortunately he did not live long enough to produce.

[2] Some words in the Latin text are partially obscured in my xerox copy of the *Astrologia Gallica*, and consequently I may have made wrong conjectures about their reading.

there is signified for him discord with his wife, or vice versa; and according to these and to other significations an opinion is brought forth about this. If the native asks whether he is going to have fortunate negotiations with another person at a proposed time, both of the nativities must be seen to see whether each is fortunate for the negotiation, and especially at that [particular] time the directions and revolutions [are fortunate], and whether the nativities of both of them agree with each other; and it must be judged on these criteria; and the procedure is the same in other cases.

For the question of the third kind. As if the native has asked when his brother will die; this in must especially be judged from the radical figure of that brother, having [also] inspected his directions and revolutions; but if that figure is not known, then the figure of the brother must be extracted from the native's figure,[1] as we have taught elsewhere, and the directions and revolutions of it should be made, and the judgment will be made from those [considerations], although with less certainty.

Next it must be noted that if the native has only this brother, the extracted figure will particularly signify him. But if he has several brothers, the extracted figure will only signify for all of them in general and not more for one than for another. There should, therefore, be little trust placed in that figure for one particular brother, but much more [trust] than in the figures of questions [made] in the manner of the Arabs, which have no foundation in nature. And the same thing must be said about a figure extracted from the nativity of a father, who has one or more children.

Nevertheless, if a question is made about the death of the native, then from figures extracted from the nativities of the father, the mother, the brothers, the spouse, etc., it is certain that diverse opinions must be derived from them, and not all of them will agree on

---

[1] This is a procedure mentioned by Ptolemy, *Tetrabiblos*, iii. 4 & 5, for extracting the horoscope of the native's father or a brother or sister by assuming that the planet signifying the person is in the ASC of a special chart. This amounts to renumbering the houses of the native's horoscope by counting them from the significator. No further details are given by Ptolemy.

the same thing. But in this case, the judgment should always be made from the figure that signifies most strongly; moreover, the personal nativity of anyone signifies most strongly [for him], but after that the figure extracted from the nativity of his father, or his son—and especially from his first born; but then [the figures extracted from] the wife and the brothers; for this is the order of power of the extracted figures; for the son shares the radical influx of the father through his generation from his father's wife, and the father lives in his children through his seed; moreover, the connection by body with his wife is greater and closer than the connection by blood with his brothers [as is established] by the Cabala of the Houses.[1]

For the questions of the fourth kind, the native's figure must not be looked at, for it influxes only on persons closely related to him; therefore, if any question is made about a unique individual not related to the native, that person's nativity should be consulted, and if that is unknown, his figure should be viewed that is extracted from his father's nativity, or his mother's, or his son's, or his spouse's, or his brother's; and the more of these that will be had, the more certain will be the judgment if they agree on the question that is propounded. But it will be much more certain if two of the extracted figures agree with the natal figure of that person.

Moreover, if anything is questioned by two men about something common to them, such as about a duel, the nativities of both of them should be consulted, then their directions and revolutions at the time of the duel, if both of them are known, or at least one of those with the extracted figures; but if both of the nativities are unknown, the opinion must be rendered from several figures extracted for each of them.

---

[1] A reference to Morin's theory of the significations of the houses originally set forth in his early book by that name, *Astrologicarum domorum cabala detecta a Joanne Baptista Morino*, 'The Cabala of the Houses Revealed by Jean Baptise Morin,' (Paris: J. Moreau, 1623). The same theory is set forth later in his *Astrologia Gallica*, Book 17.

And it must be noted, **First**, that extracted figures are also more valuable for judging more certainly of questions of the first and second kind. **Secondly**, that significators of the wife (for example) looked at in the natal figure of the native, by reason of the houses in which they are [posited], or which they rule, then their connection by body, aspect, and rulership with the significators of the native, or of other things pertaining to that [connection], signify more things properly or improperly that are common to the native and to his wife; moreover, his wife's figure extracted from the native's nativity signifies the things proper to the wife more significantly; and the reasoning is the same in other [cases].

And a figure should not be extracted from an extracted figure; otherwise the process would carry on to infinity and a constant contrariety of presages.

For questions of the fifth kind. The response must be made from figures erected at the moments of the universal constitutions, which were treated of in Book 24, for they alone suffice to render a judgment about plague, famine, floods, and similar things. But for war, it will bring forth some little bit [of information] if you inspect the natal figures of Kings and Princes, and their directions and revolutions, at the time of the current universal constitution.

Finally, for questions of the sixth kind for the administration of the Kingdom, see what we have said in opposition to Cardan in Chapter 9. For voyages then, the nativities of sailors should be viewed and those of the principal persons who undertake voyages, then the figure for the moment when the ship leaves port.[1] And for commercial ventures, the natal figures of the partners in the venture, and the figure for the hour at which the venture or the association was begun,[2] with extracted figures not neglected if natal ones are lacking.

---

[1] But here, without realizing it, Morin is recommending a Horary chart set for a time certain.

[2] And here he does it again.

Next, the doctrine set forth above requires the precautions of the Arabs, but any legitimate question can be propounded to the same astrologer a thousand times, or to a thousand astrologers at the same time or in succession. And at least from the previously stated fundamentals the same opinions must always be rendered, whether the question is about things in the past, the present, or the future, because the judgment from a true and stable doctrine is most certain. And with regard to questions propounded to an astrologer, what has been said so far should suffice.

Section II.
Astrological Elections.

Chapter 1. *What the Doctrine of Astrological Elections Involves and what the Limits of its Truth are.*

The doctrine of Elections is concerned with finding suitable times for avoiding some evil that is signified by the nativity, or feared, and acquiring something good that is promised by the nativity, or is wished for; and also for all undertakings and actions to be directed to a desired end. And so, elections differ from questions because the latter repose in the understanding of the thing quesited, but the former are directed to action.[1]

Moreover, elections can be made in two ways. **First**, by taking into account the natal figure of the person for whom the election is being made; and this method is legitimate and true. **Second**, not taking into account any natal figure, which method is illegitimate and false, as Haly proves by many reasons in Part 7, Chapter 1 of his *Judgments of the Stars*. The sum of which is that in the figure of an election of a time, even though it is apparently very fortunate, nevertheless if it is contrary to the unknown natal figure, nothing of good but rather of misfortunes will come forth from that election; for perhaps the ASC of the election will be the 8th house or the 12th of the radix, or the ruler of the ASC of the election will be the ruler of the 8th or the 12th of the radix; and it can be declared that anyone in an hour most favorable to a journey by reason of the current status of the *Caelum* may begin a journey most unfortunate to himself, either in life or in goods; while another person setting

---

[1] Not strictly true, because an election is in essence a question set for a future time, viz. "If I do it then, what will be the result?" Morin argues that a current question is only in the mind, while an election presupposes a future action. But a current question is often put to the astrologer because the Querent wishes to choose an appropriate action based on the astrologer's analysis of the chart. And a current question also often involves subsequent action, because the Querent must go to the astrologer or at least communicate with him in some way to put his question. Therefore, there is no real time distinction between questions and elections.

forth in an hour apparently most unfortunate will experience all sorts of good fortune. And that is because for some the malefic planets in their nativity are significators of life, dignities, riches, etc., when they are well disposed. Moreover, the benefic planets are significators of evil things when evilly disposed; but for others the contrary occurs. Therefore, Haly exhorts that an election should not be made for one whose nativity is not known, at least (he says) unless you have the ASC of his Question. In which already Haly is wrong when he thinks that the figure of an insubstantial Question made apart from the nativity for undertaking a journey can be the legitimate foundation of a good election for a trip.

Chapter 2. *Some things to be Generally Noted Concerning Elections.*

As for the elections of times in general, these things should be noted.

First. Those elections are beneficial not only for attaining good or for fortunately taking up anything that has been undertaken, but also for avoiding anything threatening evil or that is feared. For the one who wants to procure the friendship of a Prince or to contract a hoped for marriage, or to build a house, a castle, or a city, it makes known [how] to elect times that are especially favorable for those things, namely those in which the *Caelum* favors the Native who is undertaking such things. For the celestial influx only affects the Native primarily and per se with regard to those things that it must be said to affect by accident.

For, good fortune for constructing a house does not consist of a state of the *Caelum* as seen in the hour in which that house begins to be built (which would nevertheless be brought about if the celestial influx would primarily and per se produce an artifact), but seen with respect to the architect and the one who orders the house to be constructed; and the state of the *Caelum* could be fortunate in the first mode but unfortunate in the second mode, whence there would be bad fortune for that house, and the reasoning is the same in other cases.

Similarly, the one who wants to guard against illness threatening from the stars, having found the time of the illness by directions and by revolutions of the Sun and the Moon, would elect a time before the advent of the illness, in which he could either draw blood or safely clear away harmful humors. And a King fearing war from another King close to him, before the beginning of the war will undertake to make peace with him at a time favorable to himself for making peace, and also through men who are also at the same time fortunately disposed to this; and the reasoning is the same about an impending battle, in which goods or life will be at hazard.

Second. Anyone can, either for himself or for someone else, elect a time, both for a good or a bad end. For a good, as if someone wants to procure a dignity for his own son; but for evil, as if someone wants to ruin another person, either in his life or in his goods (which very often is permitted by bad men misusing their own power of authority), [in which case] he should wisely pay attention to his own natal figure when bad directions and Revolutions are completed. And then it will involve him in hazards, or lawsuits, or wars, or dangerous matters; and he will take it up if he has a lawsuit with him, and then he will prosper according to the stars. And the same reasoning applies to a King who will take up a war with another King. For he should not even undertake a just war, if there are [only a] few favorable directions in his nativity and some unfavorable Revolutions. And moreover it may happen the other way around for his enemy; but he would expect that there would be bad fortune for his enemies from the *Caelum*, but on the contrary he himself would receive good fortune. And it will be very profitable to consider also the nativities of the leaders of the war on both sides. And if you do not pay much attention to these,[1] usually the undertakings will turn out most unfortunately.

---

[1] Reading *his* 'these' instead of *bis* 'twice'.

Third. For any Election, such as for making a fortunate marriage contract, these two things are required: *First*, that a fortunate marriage was signified in the nativity. *Second*, that at the time of the contract there are fortunate directions, Revolutions, and transits of the significators. For with one of these lacking, the election will not be produced, however much it may seem to be opportune and favorable. For Elections cannot overthrow the things signified in the radix, nor can directions and Revolutions. Moreover, the radical signification can be of the highest, lowest, or middle degree, just as the signification chosen for the action can also be. If those things that are taken from the nativity agree with the figure of the Election to the highest degree, a great and swift effect will result, that was conformable on both sides. But if to the lowest degree, the effect will be less, or it will only be apparent. If it is in the middle degree, the effect will be middling. Moreover, the highest degree on the one side with the lowest degree on the other side, will produce more than the least effect, and with the middle degree more than the middle effect, especially if the highest degree belongs to the natal chart.

The **Fourth** and principal rule of this doctrine in practice consists of this—that those things that are going to be done are started at the moment of the figure or of the elected celestial constitution. For the whole virtue of an Election consists of the situation of the *Caelum*, which is elected to be conformable to the intended end result. Furthermore, destroyed by the diurnal motion of the *Caelum*, it also perishes or is deprived of the hoped for virtue, and that which was begun fortunately for a journey in the 9th house, is thrown into the 8th, where it portends death or dangers to life. Or, what was fortunate for health in the 1st house will cross over into the 12th, which is the house of illnesses.[1]

And therefore, in preparing to act at the elected time, everything should also be made ready before that moment, so that nothing else

---

[1] Here he is referring to the clockwise rotation of planets through the houses, such as a planet passing from the 9th house into the 8th house.

should be looked for except the moment itself, not at the common clocks, that are often wrong by more than half an hour, but by taking [the position of] the Sun or the stars. And so, having every necessary thing ready before that moment, the ruler of the said time will be rightly acquired, as the one who knew how to use it has chosen. And the figure of an Election must be dealt with thus, because it is a particular figure.

Chapter 3. *How Great the Utility of the Doctrine of Elections is.*

The doctrine of Elections is of so great utility, if it is rightly attended to, because the practical fruit of universal astrology is found to be embraced in it. For the knowledge of the stars was not given to men by God, the wisest and the best, for any reason other than that they might be able to guard against the evil things signified for them by their nativity, or to get the good things promised by the *Caelum*; and so that they might have with themselves a natural rule and direction for all their own undertakings and actions, respecting the dispensation of Divine Providence for sublunar things through the stars, and admiring the force of their own free will above the influxes of the stars, so that consequently as extensively as the field of human actions evidently is, just as extensively is [the doctrine of] Elections.

And yet, because in this obscure life the intellect of man is not capable of discerning exactly the astral causes of all his own small or medium-sized actions, and is not able to apply them correctly. I think it is safer for Elections to be used only in matters of greater moment, whose causes are more evident; and to entrust the rest to knowledge of the state of inferior things or to their supposed arrangement.

Lest someone use Elections for all kinds of business, the same thing might happen that happened to Ludovico Sforza (1452-1508), the Duke of Milan, about whom Cardan writes in *Quadripartite* Book 1, Textus 14:

"that he gambled on a money-making astrologer, but an ignorant one, and he had paid him handsomely—a hundred and more great gold talents. For which for such a price, he prescribed the time for starting such an affair. So, absurdly as if the otherwise very wise Prince would think it [proper] to mount horses in the greatest storms, and to lead his whole court and retainers through the middle of the downpours through slime and mud—just like enemies, or attackers—or to act as fugitives. I do not know whether it was from the stupidity of the astrologer, whether from great ambition, or whether from mockery, that he would ridicule the Prince himself for shame with such comments. And it happened to him (what had never happened to any other Princes of our Province) that the Kingdom was despoiled and captured by the enemy, the King of France. [The Duke] wretchedly alive in prison, also ended up confined in a box, sleeping within iron bars."[1]

With this certainly deplorable history Alexander de Angelis in his *Against the Astrologers*, Book 4, Chapter 15 tried to bring into disrepute the doctrine of Elections, rather than condemning the ignorance of a sycophantic astrologer. And it is shown that it must be feared not only by Princes, but also by any other person, especially in matters of great moment, that it is very much more dangerous to trust [in the counsel] of an ignorant astrologer, than it is to direct one's actions by the sole light of proper reason to the unknown influx of the stars. For although reason alone by itself may be ignorant of the future; nevertheless, when the future is made, the present is beginning, the reason for that is that also by reason alone it will be able either to be removed or to come to pass.

But whatever Astrology is worth, and especially the doctrine of Elections, in undertaking and managing great things, can evi-

---

[1]This refers to the Duke's capture by King Louis XII (1462-1515) of France in April of 1500. He spent the next 8 years confined in an underground dungeon at Loches, France, where he died on 17 May 1508.

dently be conjectured from the more secret Council of the King of China—to which only 12 men of the whole Kingdom are admitted—but no one of them is admitted who is not an outstanding astrologer. Because indeed in that Council the stars are consulted first about things to be done, rather than about the persons who are to be put in charge of those things, and about the times that are suitable for doing those things. But nevertheless, the men most skilled in political matters would not act with one voice, unless they would know from experience that that thing would lead to the ruling of the people. And the same thing was common to the first monarchs of the World, who in difficult matters used to consult their own mages—not so called for any reason other than for their skill in astrology, which is the sublime and divine science.

And I indeed think that for a King or a Prime Minister there is scarcely anything that would be more useful than in fact a council of three very skilled astrologers, who would have the true nativities not only of the Kings and his close Princes but also of all the notable Magnates of the court and those aspiring to dignities; for then from which King and when, war could be avoided; against whom and when it would be undertaken, and those who would be selected as leaders of the armed forces, and those who would be passed over, and it would not be known without the enjoyment of decoration; when on the contrary very often a war might be undertaken by a very unfortunate King, and one that led to the dispersing of his Kingdom rather than to its flourishing; and that in a very unfortunate year for that King, and by ruinous military leaders; against the King then another fortunate time. From which occurrences, could nothing but a great disaster be expected? Moreover, what is said here about war can similarly be said about the health and the marriage of the King, about sending legations or receiving them, and about other important affairs of the Kingdom. Moreover, I would recommend at least three astrologers, for one might not be equal to that burden; while two would disagree with each other; but three should certainly be appointed, since in many instances of quarreling over controversies of little moment, may times more judges are admitted. And no one should think that this was said on my account—I who would without doubt reject such duty; for if in my youth I had held the court in dislike, as something inimical to my freedom and personal integrity; and I rather fled [from it] instead of courting Princes or being subject to Magnates. It is certain that now that I am 66 years of age[1] and not far from the end of my life, the immeasurably corrupt atmosphere of the court strongly makes me sick; and I would be insane if I did not reflect on death rather than on life in the court. But let it only be said that, thanks to the truth and dignity of Astrology, by which, when I am gone, the excellence of Astrology itself will become known from this work.

But if Astrology is useful and necessary for Kings and Princes in the greatest affairs, and this part of it especially, no one can have any doubt that it can also be useful to other men of any degree for undertaking individual works of any sort fortunately—whether it pertains to agriculture, the begetting of children or domestic animals, or the taking of medicine, or to any sort of human dealings. And then, to avoiding unfortunate positions of the *Caelum*, under which great evils or dangers are accustomed to occur—especially in those years in which there are bad directions and revolutions, as we have abundantly proved by 8 celestial figures in Book 24, Section 2, Chapter 11 at the moment of the beginning of the battle[2] in which Gustavus Adolphus (1594-1632) the King of Sweden fell, of the death of some men, and of the great dangers in which he himself was.

---

[1] Since Morin was born in 1583, he was writing this in 1649, which may indicate the year in which he completed the first draft of the *Astrologia Gallica*. But he had yet another 7 years of life remaining, and he may have rewritten some earlier portions of the book, but in the main he evidently completed it in 1649. Also, he continued writing on various subjects to the end of his life—most notably producing a work in French, his *Remarques Astrologiques*, a translation and commentary on Ptolemy's *Centiloquy*, written in opposition to *Le Centilogve de Ptolomee* by Nicolas Bourdin, the Marquis de Villennes, that was published in 1651. Like the *Astrologia Gallica*, the *Remarques Astrologiques* was unfortunately not published until after Morin's death in 1656.

[2] The Battle of Lützen, Germany, which took place on 16 November 1632. See Book 23 for further details.

But because as often neither the King, nor his Prime Minister, nor any other men are taking care to compare their natal figures with those of those with whom they are going to have a meeting. Therefore, with the elections of times not standing in the way of acting harmonious according to the nativity of the King, or of his Prime Minister, it may occasionally be that the hoped for effect does not follow; for the Minister has hanging over himself the fortune or misfortune of the King that he serves. Moreover, the King and the Minister have beneath themselves the fortune or misfortune of those men who carry out their orders or whom they employ to bring them to completion. Moreover, the personal fortune or misfortune of the King or the Minister depends upon those persons in the common concourse. And therefore, all these things must be inspected and mixed together for a truer prediction of events even so, and the influences of many Planets on the same occurrence of events. But if the nativities of the other persons are unknown, it will only have to be said that the stars of the King himself or those of his Prime Minister give the particular forebodings in that year by their directions and the revolution, then on the very day or hour by the Election. For it is better to know this than not to know it, and it will produce boldness in prescribing or applying cautions for other unknown things.

And the same thing must be judged about the Commander in Chief of any army, and then about all those who serve someone else's will, or who entrust their own action to another—especially in actions of major moment, but it is better to know one's own *Caelum*, and then to favor it, rather than to do the contrary. For, of the two Commanders or Kings battling in turn, if either of them will know from the hour of the beginning of the battle that the *Caelum* is propitious for him; he will rightly doubt whether he is not equal to the enemy, or is more so; and therefore he will fight more boldly—although it would be safer to have the nativity of the enemy, and by the inspection of both of them to elect a *Caelum* opportune for himself, but at the same time one contrary to the enemy. For then, victory will certainly be hoped for the King who the

Caelum favors, provided that there is due cooperation from a fortunate influx of that *Caelum*.

In fact, it must be known from the things that the celestial bodies are particularly signifying to someone, whatever sort of things they are, that the Native has contributed nothing of his own, and that he holds himself merely passively, so that when something unexpected falls from on high, or when he falls among armed robbers, or when he receives a benefice from the King, or a promotion to a dignity, about which he was not even thinking. And these occurrences occur to the Native solely from a malefic or a benefic influx of the stars. But there are others even so when the stars alone seem to arouse the Native, but they do not cause them alone; but those require the cooperation of the Native himself, whatever kinds of things are undertaken—battles, business affairs, and all actions that are particular to the Native himself. For just as the *Caelum* is in nature a most perfect image of God in his mode of acting—just as has been shown elsewhere—so, the natural influx is very similar to the supernatural influx of God that is called *grace*. For just as by his own grace God excites the will to acting, but He does not compel it, or subject it to Himself, nor does He all alone performs an action, but the cooperation of the man is required. And when the cooperation of the man is conformable to the influx of the Stars, the event happens—whether it is good or evil—according to the quality of the influx. But if the man's cooperation is contrary to the influx, or even if he does not cooperate, the influence will have no effect upon him properly and per se.

But hence it is plain that those who confide too much on astrology are very much deceived when they believe that the good fortune signified for them by the stars in their undertakings and actions will come to pass, even if they do nothing, or if they act inappropriately—thinking that it is sufficient that because the *Caelum* has signified it, it should certainly come to pass. And if it doesn't come to pass, they conclude that either astrology is false, or else they have been deceived by an astrologer. For an astrologer in predicting good fortune from the stars for undertakings or actions freely taken by the Native, supposes a conformable collaboration by the native himself, who can by his own discretion avoid a predicted evil, but so by his own negligence or indiscretion lose the good promised to him by the *Caelum*. And the astrologer is not held to respond by the success of his own prediction, but only by a prediction made according to art or the influx of the stars. Truly, since the stars incline men—and to what they incline them can be predicted—but what may come to pass from their free actions can only be predicted conjecturally. Since with regard to these things, astrology is for the human intellect only a conjectural science. Then, on account of the indifference of free will to anything particular; and then on account of the concourse of other causes that are also mostly free, but to what extent they are affected by the *Caelum* is not known. For even if the greater part of men follow their own innate propensities (which can be predicted safely); nevertheless, there are many who either by prudence, or religion, or compulsion, or captivity escape the influxes of the stars. And it must be more cautiously predicted about these persons, by taking into account their condition or status, so that it should be apparent to everyone how much sagacity is required of the astrologer in predicting, and because nothing can be defined for certain or infallibly with regard to free actions, but only conjecturally. Nevertheless, with the greater probability that things will be signified more probably by the *Caelum*. But always warning those men who are greedy for predictions that the *Caelum* does indeed presage such things for certain, but their effects principally depend on cooperation—either for evil or for good. Moreover, with the things just said duly noted, and how much can be done for the things watched in electing a suitable time for doing things, it can scarcely be doubted that a great utility will frequently come out of that.

Chapter 4. *How Vain the Arguments of Alexander de Angelis against Elections are.*

Alexander de Angelis, *Against the Astrologers*, Book 4, Chapter 15, has many futile arguments against Elections, with which he applauds himself. But none of them are worth commenting on except for these two arguments, by which with fatal schemes he thinks that he has overthrown this part of astrology and therefore the entirety of astrology.

The *First one* is like this:

> "Either the natal stars by a vow promise the thing that you have undertaken (he is addressing an astrologer) will be fortunate, or unfortunate and inauspicious, or else the natal horoscope has nothing to do with it. If the former, by whatever star that you have undertaken the thing, you will handle the business with a fortunate and favorable outcome. If the latter, no stars will avail you against the natal decrees. If the things do not pertain to the natal stars, every natal teaching, that deduces everything from the stars that preside over conception and birth, fails."

But, having passed over the last two clauses, I reply to the first. That gives evidence very plainly of Alexander de Angelis's ignorance of astrology. For indeed he did not know that the natal stars promise fortunate things, but not at just any time, but certainly and definitely that they are measured by directions and confirmed by conformable revolutions. And because in birth the celestial figure is suited to the constitution of the fetus; it marvelously leads it out of the uterus into the mundane scene, and it puts it under its own jurisdiction and subjects it to itself influentially. So, a good signified by the nativity, and by a direction and a revolution that has matured conformably, a conformable celestial figure through the position of the *Caelum* and suitable transits of the Planets, is brought across from potential to action; and it makes that appear which is very true and a genuine foundation of Elections.

Besides, he does not know that since in every nativity both good things and evil things are signified (for there is no nativity that is altogether happy or unlucky), it is absurd to suppose that either all things are good at the same time or all things are evil at the same time, or that all things good and evil happen to the Native at the same time. For when would everything happen at once? And what [then] would happen in the remaining time of life? Or why would it be good rather than evil? Or on the contrary why would it happen at a certain time? Therefore, it must be acknowledged that whatever you please of good or evil happens in its own time, as is proved by directions; and consequently, it is false that whatever thing you are going to undertake by a certain star (that is, at a certain time), you will handle the thing with a successful and favorable outcome.

The *Second one* is like this:

> "But let us make in the condition of the *Caelum* to take in hand some path by which to choose a path by which nothing more lucky can be desired. would the constitution of this sort of *Caelum* endure during the whole time of a very long journey? Therefore the *Caelum* ought to stand still as long as the men are moving, and who could put up with nonsense of that sort? Perhaps with time it will vanish? By which mode will it just preserve a long journey of many days and also of months? Or is it going to say that a man is affected by the stars, when he first mounts a horse, and that he is affected and preserved to endure for the whole time of his life to provide good fortune? But really? The one who is making the journey, does he not get up on his horse every day? Why is he not affected by other [configurations] and by the other daily [configurations], which follow after them in the [sequential] rulership of sublunar things? But already if diversely on individual days—indeed, on individual hours—he is affected—why does either a lucky or an unlucky prognostication come forth. And the astrologers will not explain that—how a journey extends the path of an acting star, driving away from the road armed robbers, the [stars] temper the heat of the

Sun with scattered clouds, they support the horses lest they come to grief, they level out the mountains and valleys, all of which things must occur if a prosperous journey can occur."

These things are good for a laugh, and I wanted to add some things unworthy of a learned man, as it is plain that Alexander de Angelis was unacquainted with what a prosperous journey consists of. Therefore, I ask of him whether the journey of the Most Blessed Virgin Mary to visit Elizabeth was prosperous and fortunate? And yet she made that through the mountains of Judea, according to Luke, Chapter 1, which were not leveled like the mountains Sepher, Gadgad, Hor,[1] and Abarim,[2] in which the Children of Israel laid out camps in their journey from Egypt into the Promised Land, Numbers Chapter 33. Whether all journeys through mountains are unlucky, but those are only lucky that are on the plains, which are accustomed to be chosen for battles, in which one part of the battlers always experiences misfortune? And why too didn't De Angelis say that the *Caelum* ought to divide the seas and rivers, as they were divided in the journey of the Children of Israel?

Consequently, it is not in these that the good fortune of a journey consists, but in this—that beginning a journey with fortunate health, without any bizarre or extraordinary obstacles that could not be overcome, and without the loss of his own baggage when he arrives at the desired place—that is the goal of the journey. But as for that which De Angelis queries—whether the elected constitution of the *Caelum* would last for the whole time of the longest journey? and that it cannot be true that the *Caelum* would stand still as long as the men are being moved—I reply that that same absurdity can be asked about the celestial figure, under which someone is said to be fortunately born, which indeed would not endure in the World through the quiet of the *Caelum* as long as the Native

---

[1] The Latin text has 'Jor', but Numbers 33,41 has 'Hor' for the name of the mountain.

[2] The spelling of these geographical names varies in the modern English translations of the Bible.

lives, but it does endure in the Native through its impression on him; and it endures in the *Caelum* through its determination.

And so when De Angelis asks whether you are going to say that a man is affected by the stars when he first mounts his horse, and he is affected and preserved to endure the whole time of his life, and to be provided good fortune? I reply that the matter has itself thus. And it is mere nonsense and empty words, which are said to the contrary by De Angelis. For in the *Caelum* and man's sympathy, the natal constitution of the *Caelum* is a rule for the rest of the things of the man himself. For just as a man in his own nativity is generally subjected to any determined influx of the stars for his whole life, and he does not assume a new subjection day by day, as is proved by experience in his habits, his intelligence, and his mode of action, so when he begins anything that is not alien to his own natal figure and conforming to a direction and a revolution, through the figure of an Election suited to a particular moment he undertakes a thing, he receives an actual influx from the *Caelum* that is particular and similar to the potential of his radix for accomplishing that very thing. Which, by consequence lasts until the thing itself may be perfected, and it is not changed day by day. For otherwise, there would be no influx for *doing* anything, but only for *beginning* it. And if day by day or hour by hour the influx relating to that thing should be changed, certainly since the celestial influx both from the *Caelum* and also from the planets varies the motion repeatedly, either nothing would be perfected, or it would progress very inordinately; and so the radical figure would be false in everything, because despite in long journeys that were fortunate according to the figure of the *Election*, it will evidently be false and less than that. And the logic is the same in other cases.

Much more seriously would this objection of ours be if the *Caelum* should not only signify future events happening to the Native, but also the particular times of those events by revolutions and directions, as we have stated many times elsewhere. Therefore, either the *Caelum* will effect those things that it has signified for those times, or it will not effect them. And moreover, whatever you may have said, the Election of days and hours will be useless and ineffective.

But I reply. The decrees of the *Caelum* are not a fatal necessity, especially in freely-chosen actions, but they depend in their own effects on the cooperation by man, which indeed they do excite at a certain time, but they do not determine them; and that time has a certain latitude, as was said at the end of Section I, Chapter 3, during which a man can determine himself to act. Moreover, since during that time the places of the planets are continually being changed; and the face of the *Caelum* varies much hour by hour, it cannot be denied that an action undertaken—such as a long journey—could most conveniently be accommodated to the *Caelum*, or the *Caelum* to the action as much as possible, which will always be the best and most fortunate [procedure]. And yet this can only be done by means of Elections. Therefore, they are most useful, and indeed necessary for the more fortunate outcome of the thing undertaken.

Chapter 5. *What Cardan Thought about Elections.*

Cardan was stumbling on Elections, so that he only fell flat. For in his little treatise *On Questions*, in Question 14 he says:

> "it is seen that Elections are useful; namely, when carved or established[1] at an influx of the *Caelum*, they seem to do something for pains and stone in the kidneys; not because it is such a figure, for either the dog or the lion or the mountain you will have carved at that hour will be the same; but because it is an action that can [do] something by an Election."

But Cardan even wishes to avoid superstition by [the use of]

---

[1] Here Cardan is referring to an *astrological image* that was made at a time chosen by an Election. These were what we would call "good luck charms," and they were made to bring good fortune to some particular thing in the Client's life.

such words; nevertheless, he will remain impure by that, when he approves of such remedies for illnesses.

Besides, if something sculpted heals, to what extent is anything done under such an election, or an earthen vessel, or a wooden one, or a walk, or a speech, etc., able to provide a remedy from kidney pains and stone, to what extent is the action with such an Election, which it is ridiculous to suppose Besides, we have proved that elsewhere, and in Section 1, Chapter 3, we have said that such things are not susceptible per se to the celestial influx.

Cardan also adds:

> "In a monarchy an Election does something, but not according to the day." And in Chapter 22 of his *Book on the Judgments of Nativities* he says: "In the beginnings of things an Election does something, but in voluntary things it is of little use and it is very difficult, and an Election of days and hours is most absurd, with the exception of natural things, such as sowing, pruning, and similar things, since in things free so far of perfection" he says "we have not come to [the point] where we can arrive at the decrees of the days; and therefore in these" he exclaims "who will know how to make an Election?" And in the place on Elections cited above he concludes "that if anyone is fortunate in voluntary things, it results from nature and the year; if he is unfortunate, he breaks and rebuffs, not only the convenient time, but also very often the thing itself."

These are Cardan's opinions about Elections. In which, however, he is here and there greatly at odds not only with himself but with all astrologers. For why are directions and revolutions, progressions and transits admitted into this art, unless so that favorable and unfavorable days and hours may be found and the good or evil things signified by them may be foretold; which we have read has been declared by many persons, and concerning whom Cardan prides himself in his *Book on Revolutions*, then Giacopo Maria of Ferrara, and then Paride Ceresario (c.1466-c.1532),[1] and he hands down that he was familiar with those famous astrologers of his own time?

And would not astrological science be very imperfect, if indeed from the nativity there could be predicted the danger of a violent death at some time in the future, but not the year, or the month, or the day? Or if the year [could be predicted], but not the month, or if the month [could be predicted], but not the day? And the Native will not be tormented during the whole month or year; and in vain would he be in fear before the time of the danger, but, with it impending, should he neglect taking care of himself?

And are unlucky accidents observed to happen on fortunate days, but lucky ones on unfortunate days? I have certainly never observed this, but always the other way around. And more than a hundred times I was sorry that I had not predicted great good or evil things that would happen to Magnates or Princes whose nativities I had, and which I could have predicted to the very day, as I have predicted in some instances, for in fact there were evident and potent causes on those days. But predictions of that sort—or at least frequent ones—only belong to that astrologer, who, as Cardan himself warns in Chapter 22, has nothing else to do, and will take pains with all of his practice, which certainly never happens to me. For, through almost continual distractions and various kinds of hindrances during 30 years, I was devoted to constructing, purifying, and confirming the Theory [of astrology].

But although this particular prediction may be difficult—pertaining in particular to the annual and monthly revolutions and their directions, and then to the transits of the planets, which were discussed in detail in Books 23 and 24, yet it is far from being said

---

[1] See Thorndike, HMES, V, 256. He seems to have been a native of Mantua. He was said to have predicted to Cardinal Alessandro Farnese (1468-1549) that he would become Pope, which occurred 12 years later in 1534, when he became Pope Paul III.

to be impossible, and I hope that by the Theory—now that it is properly constructed—such predictions will be very frequent among those of us who have understood the doctrine hitherto set forth by us. For even though Cardan in that Chapter 22 boasts that he has discovered this science, yet when he exclaims, "who would know how to elect?" and when he says that "the Election of days and hours in unrestricted things is most absurd," he shows that his knowledge about this matter was meager, since an Election does not harm anything of free will, but rather it is consistent with free will, and it complements it. But let what we have said so far about these matters suffice.

Chapter 6. *General Rules Necessary for Elections. And in what Way an Election Should be Made for any Particular Thing.*

Having set forth those things that we have previously said, now it seems that some general rules that are necessary for elections must be added, by which it will be shown how in general an election must be made for any particular thing. Moreover, we have chosen these rules from various authors, especially from the Arabs,[1] from among the many unreliable rules, with which they are confusedly mixed; and we have arranged them in order for the greater facility of learning and using them, also we have accommodated many of them to our own principles. Furthermore, it must be noted that not from these things looked at simply and absolutely should the rules for Elections be established, as many of the Arabs and their followers make them, but always with regard to the figure of the nativity, and those things that depend upon it at the time of the Election—namely, the radical directions, the revolutions of the Sun and the Moon, and their directions, as well as their transits. Therefore, let it be:

---

[1] Here, after having severely criticized the Arabs in Section I, he selects many of their rules. But he does modify them to bring them into agreement with his insistence on using them in connection with the indications of the natal chart of the person making the election.

First. Every legitimate Election should be made by inspecting the nativity, its revolutions, directions, and the transits of the planets through the places of the nativity and its revolutions, and by accommodating the individual considerations as much as can be done to the goal of the election.

Second. See to which house of the figure the matter pertains for which the Election is to be made. As, if it is about dignity, it pertains to the 10th; if about a wife, to the 7th; if about a journey, to the 9th or to the 3rd; etc. And if the Election should be made for obtaining a dignity, Schöner[1] and others elect a time when the progressions of the ASC, the MC, and the Sun and Moon of the radix, will be in the 10th of the radix. But because progressions were rejected by us in Book 24,[2] therefore you should elect a time when the *directions* of the ASC, the MC, the Sun and the Moon, and their rulers in the revolutions of the Sun and the Moon, would come to the 10th of the radix, or to a favorable aspect of it, or to a benefic planet in it, or to the ruler of that house, or to their fortunate aspects. And on the day when that will occur most fortunately, elect an appropriate hour—that is, when the position of the *Caelum* is suitable for your goal, and then erect the figure. And the procedure is the same for starting a journey, or contracting a marriage, etc.

Third. In the figure of an Election, special attention must be paid to the ASC of the person for whom the Election is being made, and also to the MC, which signifies his undertakings and actions, and to the house of the figure to which the thing for which the Election is being made pertains. And also the Moon, which in all Elections is rightly important—namely, so that in the figure of the Election it should be well disposed. And take care if the places of the ASC, the MC, and the Moon should be badly disposed in the nativity, or the cusps of the evil houses, but rather well disposed, or the cusps of the good and appropriate houses.

---

[1]Johann Schöner (1477-1547), German mathematics professor and astrologer.
[2]By 'progressions' Morin refers to what are properly called *profections* (symbolic progressions), not to progressions (directions) that have an astronomical basis.

Fourth. See to it that the house of the figure of the election which pertains to the thing for which the Election is being made is well disposed at the hour of the election. But if in the figure of the radix it is also well disposed, and also in the figure of the current revolutions of both the Sun and the Moon, that will be best. Moreover, it will be fortified in effectiveness or by the rulership of the benefics, that also in both the radix and the revolutions would be benefic by nature, and well disposed; and determined by body, by rulership, or by an aspect conformable to the thing for which the Election is made. But if the Election is for a dignity, and in the figure of the election the sign of the 10th [house] of the radix or of the current revolution will have culminated, or else that sign in which the ruler of that house was posited is in the 10th, the Election will be all the better and more effective; and similarly with other [Elections]. Moreover, you will take especial care lest a planetary nature or radical determination that is malefic and contrary to the goal be in that same house of the election. And you will try to have a benefic planet posited in it, or else its ruler, that is fortunate in its rulership, or connected by aspect with the ASC or the MC or with their rulers.

Fifth. In personal things—that is, things relating to him alone—make the ASC of the Election be the ASC of his own nativity. But in common things—that is, those in which you require the aid of friends—make the cusp of the 11th or the 5th of the radix be the ASC of the Election. That is Schöner's recommendation, but why in common things being done with the exertion of friends, for the ASC of the Election to be the cusp of the radix put as its ASC, rather than the ASC of the radix? Because, if the ASC of the radix should be put, then the ASC of every Election ought to be the ASC of the radix, because everything that must be done is either personal or common, but that is not required. And consequently, since the ASC of the election always signifies the one for whom the Election is made, I think it should be noted that at least that one should be well disposed with the ruler of the house of the radix to which the matter pertains for which the Election is made, or else with a planet that is present in the house itself. And let the ruler of the 11th be well disposed, or a planet that is in it, if the work of friends is needed for that thing, or if the Election is for conciliating friendship. And the procedure is the same with the other [types of Elections].

Sixth. In electing the ASC of a figure of Election, the nature of the thing for which the Election is being made must be taken into account—namely, so that the ASC may be appropriate for that thing. And therefore for a thing that you want to be done quickly, such as a journey, make a mobile sign ascend and avoid a fixed sign. But for a thing that you want to last, such as a marriage, or building a house, choose a fixed sign and avoid a mobile one. And take care that the ruler of the ASC is not slow, retrograde, or afflicted by malefics, and especially that it is not applying to them.

Seventh. By day make the ASC sign to be a diurnal sign, and by night a nocturnal one. and also, let the Sun by day be in a diurnal sign; and by night let the Moon be in a nocturnal one. And let the Ruler of the ASC be correctly posited with respect to the Sun or the Moon; for an Election will be better and more effective when diurnal planets are above the Earth by day, in masculine signs, and oriental to the Sun; and when nocturnal planets are above the Earth by night, in feminine signs, and occidental to the Moon.

Eighth. If the Ruler of the ASC of the Election is the Ruler of the ASC of the radix, or of the current revolution and is benefic by nature, and well disposed on both sides, it will be very fortunate in the Election.

Ninth. If anything will be sought from a King, or a Queen, or a Prince, or some kind of Magnate, or for a Dignity, or in dealing with such men, adjust the ASC and its ruler to the Ruler of the MC of the radix and the revolution, and also to the analogous planets—that is, the Sun for a King, the Moon for a Queen, Jupiter for a Chancellor, Chief Officer, or Bishop, Mars for a General, and so on with the rest. And if an analogous planet is the Ruler of the MC, it will be more effective. But take care that it is not badly disposed in the radix or the revolution, or that it is determined to evil things. And the rule is the same for other persons pertaining to houses 3, 4, 5, 7, and 9.

Tenth. All the old astrologers give as much force to the Moon in Elections, as if they would have it pertain if not primarily, at least secondarily to the [purpose of] the Election. And yet I do not see that they give any consideration to its determination in the radical figure, yet nevertheless that observation seems to me altogether necessary, unless if it was the significator of death in the nativity, it might be assumed to be the significator of life in the election, or some appropriate precaution. And this must be considered not only in the case of the Moon, but in the case of any of the planets. Moreover, the old astrologers say the following things about the Moon.

Eleventh. The Native should not begin anything new when the Moon is in the radical place of Saturn or Mars, or in their bad aspects, or in a sign that is badly afflicted in the nativity, or in the 6th, 8th, or 12th house of the nativity. And similarly, in the figure of an Election take care that it not be afflicted by Saturn, or by Mars, by body, or by aspect, and that it not be in the 6th, 8th, or 12th. Indeed, it should not be in the 1st, as almost all [the astrologers] will have it, because (as they say) it might be inimical to the ASC on account of its coldness, which I think is a groundless reason, except perhaps in medicine or agriculture, and even then only occasionally.

Twelfth. The applications of the Moon to Mars from the domiciles of Venus, and to Jupiter from the domiciles of Mercury, and to the Sun from the domiciles of Saturn must be avoided. And consequently, take care lest this occur in the figure of an Election.

Thirteenth. The Moon conjunct Saturn or Jupiter, and increased in light and number[1] will be good for everything; but if she

---

[1] "Increased in number" = "swift."

has little light, it will be evil for everything. But understand the contrary of all this, when she will be joined to Mars or Venus.

Fourteenth. Take careful note of the Moon's place in the figure of an Election. For if she is in trine or sextile to any radical planet, it will be safe to act with those persons that the planet will signify both by its own nature and by its radical determination. But if it is in square or opposition to the planet. it will act in a contrary manner. For example, if the Moon is trine the radical Mars, especially if it is the 7th of the radix, or if it is the ruler of the 7th and well disposed, victory in battle or in a lawsuit will be signified, and also the favor of soldiers, cavalrymen, and the governmental army, or the favor of administrators and attorneys in lawsuits. But if she is in square or opposition, it will be the other way around. And the rule is the same for other configurations.

Fifteenth. The Moon well located in the house of the thing for which the Election is being made—for example, in the 9th, if the Election is being made for a journey—provided that it is in a place that is fortunate in the radix, and which if it also signified that very thing, and the Moon herself also signified the same thing; and in addition she is also aspecting a well disposed ASC, or ruling it, nothing more fortunate could be desired.

Sixteenth. Take care that the Moon is not joined to a retrograde planet or is applying to it. For the thing that is undertaken will be destroyed.

Seventeenth. If you cannot fortify the Moon and the ASC at the same time, rather then by day fortify the ASC, but by night the Moon. And if by day she is under the Earth, and by night above the Earth, it will be better for the ASC.

Eighteenth. Take note of the conjunction or the opposition of the Lights[1] preceding the Election—namely, so that their place in the figure of the Election is a fortune one, and in an appropriate house.

---

[1] That is, the New Moon or the full Moon.

Nineteenth. When the Moon is separated from Mars, or is opposite the Sun, and applies to a malefic, especially when it is determined to evil in the nativity, beware of starting anything—at least, anything of importance. For that time is very evil; and it will be worse if she applies to its square or opposition.

Twentieth. From the good or evil state of the place of Mars or the opposition of the Lights preceding the Election; and the state of the benefic or malefic planet to which the Moon immediately applies, the outcome of the thing for which the Election is being made may be conjectured. For if the state of the place is good and the planet is a benefic, the thing will proceed fortunately from the beginning to the end. But if the state of the place is evil and the planet is a malefic, the thing will proceed unfortunately from the beginning to the end—or it will not be done at all. If the state of the place is good, and the planet is a malefic, the thing will begin well and end evilly. Finally, if the state of the place is evil, and the planet is benefic, the thing will begin evilly but it will end well.

Twenty-first. When an Election is urgent, and there is not time to check that all the significators are well suited [to the thing]. Then in fact it must at least be adjusted so that the Ruler of the ASC is well suited to it, and a benefic is in an angle with a fortunate aspect to the ASC.

Twenty-second. In every Election that requires haste, if you cannot fortify the Moon, then put Jupiter or Venus, in the ASC, or in the MC, but put the Moon in a cadent house. And beware of letting a malefic aspect the ASC, especially by a malign aspect, or a planet that by its own nature or by its radical determination signifies the thing for which the election is being made – or their rulers, or the ruler of the house to which the thing itself pertains.

Twenty-third. In an urgent Election, with no time given for checking how far all the significators can be appropriately adjusted, at least adjust the ASC and the MC so that they are well adapted [to the thing]; and let there be benefics in the angles favorably aspecting the ASC, or the MC, or their rulers. Indeed, it must be noted that it rarely happens in Elections that you can adapt all the significators as you would like; but always look to see what can be done that is better and more appropriate for your goal; and provide that, and whatever else your own prudence may supply. Remember that the cooperation of man with the stars [is needed], and the lazier or the more careless he is, the less can be hoped for from the stars. But the more diligent, and stronger, and wiser he is, the more can be hoped for.

Twenty-fourth. In every Election take care that the malefics are not in the angles, and especially in the ASC and the MC, unless by their celestial state and determination they were [acting as] benefics in the radix. For then you can use them for good. Nevertheless, it must be noted that malefics are very useful for things of their own nature—such as Mars for battles, victories, hunting, and lawsuits; and Saturn for building houses, agriculture, etc. And especially if they were determined to such things in the radix.

Twenty-fifth. A consideration of the fixed stars—especially the brighter ones—should by no means be omitted in Elections. For in the angles and with the significators they can produce notable effects, especially if they should also have been determined in the radix to the thing for which there is a question.

And from the general Aphorisms set above for all Elections, it should be sufficiently plain how an Election should be made for any particular thing that at least pertains to the things signified by the 12 celestial houses; although there are some particular things, for which some specific Aphorisms are appropriate—which are, for example, those that follow.

Twenty-sixth. You should not cut any bodily part with iron when the Moon is in the sign that is ruled by that part.

Twenty-seventh. In purgings use the Moon when she is in water signs, and especially Scorpio or Pisces. And let the Ruler of the ASC be connected to a planet under the Earth—especially in applying, he may vomit up the potion; and also its force may be weakened if the Moon is conjoined to Jupiter, or if it is in Leo, or an earth sign.

Twenty-eighth. When going on a journey, take care lest the 8th house and its ruler be afflicted; and do not let a fixed sign ascend, nor let the Ruler of the ASC be a malefic, retrograde, or the Moon be badly afflicted. For the more of these there are, the more unfortunate the journey will be.

Twenty-ninth. You should not go out to battle when the Ruler of the ASC is especially weak or afflicted, or when it will go to the ruler of the 7th—especially if it is strong or in the 8th—or when the Moon is badly afflicted.

Thirtieth. When you are going to ask anything of a King, or a Queen, or Magnates, put the Sun or the Moon with Jupiter or Venus well disposed in the 10th, and well connected with the ruler of the ASC; and you will get [what you are asking for].

But these should now be sufficient, for many more things will be said concerning the practice of astrology, provided that God gives us time.[1] And it will only be noted here that a careful election of times is not a task for just any astrologer, but only for a very learned and wise one, who must not only pay attention to the state and disposition of the inferior causes—namely, so that they may be prepared for the elected hour. And this to be sure is easy for those things that are within our power, such as starting a journey; but in things that are not within our power, as in addressing a King on a selected day and hour, that will be more difficult in many cases, and it can scarcely be done except by the dear mediations of friends, who offer access to the King at that very hour. Therefore, these causes must first be arranged for the elected hour; and it will have to be done similarly in other instances.

---

[1] This refers to a book that Morin often mentions that he intends to write dealing specifically with the practice of astrology. But either he never wrote it, or it was never published.

Chapter 7. *In which the Use of Elections is Shown and Proved by two Notable Examples.*

Elections of years, days, and hours can be made that are of notable utility. For if someone has been made fortunate with dignities, he will foresee that in some year with a completed direction of the MC to the Sun, or to Jupiter Ruler of the ASC or the MC he may safely elect that year for providing a dignity for himself, and combining harmoniously with the celestial influx—especially if in that year there is a favorable revolution of the Sun; for even if he ignores the month, day, and hour in a year, that is more prosperous for his intention. Nevertheless, persistently in working with celestial fate, he will implement the things promised by himself. But if he does not ignore those things, then it may occur with a favoring *Caelum*, with much less labor, and his wish will be accomplished more happily.

I could offer many more examples here to show and prove the use of Elections from our own observations; but the two that follow should suffice—warning those for whom they might not suffice, that from the doctrine handed down by us they were relying on other observations.

Therefore, in the year 1646 around the middle of spring. the most illustrious Lord Léon de Bouthillier (1608-1652), Count of Chavigny, Antibes, etc., the second Minister of the Kingdom of France, along with the eminent Cardinal Mazarin (1602-1661), wanted to undertake a long journey to his County Antipolis—in French, Antibes—a fortified city and port on the Mediterranean Sea, at the extreme southeastern part of France, at least 200 French leagues[1] distant from the city of Paris. And out of his benevolence he invited me to [accompany him on] that journey. I delayed my response to what [would be] for me a long journey, and I had most

---

[1] The old French league was equivalent to 2.08 statute miles, so 200 leagues would be 416 statute miles. The actual straight line distance between Paris and Antibes is 431 statute miles, but they went by a roundabout way that was probably near 500 statute miles.

carefully inspected the stars that were presaging ill health for me in that same year; and finally I did agree [to go]. But I asked that most illustrious and very intelligent Lord, and a man cultivated in every kind of learning, and not alien to astrology, that it would please me to elect the day and the hour to make a fortunate departure, which would be a test of great moment to begin something that was undertaken under a conformable state of the *Caelum*. And so when the most illustrious Lord, very fond of knowing things, had approved with a pleasing mind, and had decided to depart soon, I elected 7:09 AM of 9 May. But I warned him to take care that everything was ready to go, so that at that very moment he could embark on the trip; and that was done by him most diligently and accurately. And in fact in his very beautiful garden, with the Sun shining on an outstanding clock with the sundial illuminated almost by the half hour that we had waited for—the elected moment of time; at which instant, with everything having been made ready, he embarked on his journey and set out from Paris with around 30 persons and that number of horses.

Now we may inspect the figures and the status of the *Caelum*, both for the most illustrious Lord and for me [see page 80].

These [figures] and the following nativity are not from the commons, as at first glance is plain to any astrologer. But the first one is distinguished by good [positions]; but the second one is indeed distinguished by evils; the decrees of which we have explained in judging hundreds of illustrious nativities that have been drawn up by us. Here, let it suffice that in the nativity of the most illustrious Lord Count of Chavigny the Sun and Mercury, are rulers of the 9th house, the Moon is in the 9th house, Jupiter is the Ruler of the ASC and the 3rd, conjunct the Sun and Mercury, trine the cusp of the 9th; and Mars rules the Sun, Mercury, and Jupiter, and is trine the Moon; then, Venus is in the 3rd, and Saturn her ruler, are significators of travels, but especially the Moon, the Sun, Mercury, Jupiter, and Venus. Many journeys and also long travels were signified by them.

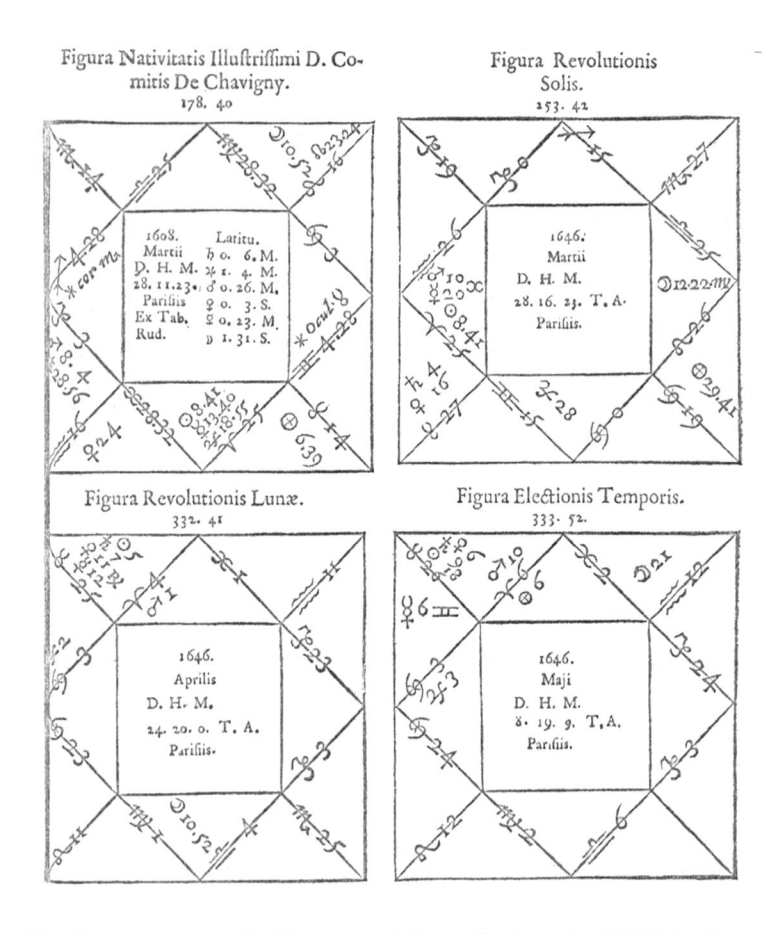

Figura Nativitatis Illuſtriſſimi D. Comitis De Chavigny.
178. 40

1608.   Latitu.
Martii   ♄ 0. 6. M.
D. H. M. ♃ 1. 4. M.
28, 11.23. ♂ 0. 26. M.
Pariſiis ♀ 0. 3. S.
Ex Tab. ☿ 0. 23. M.
Rud.   ☽ 1. 31. S.

Figura Revolutionis Solis.
253. 42

1646.
Martii
D. H. M.
28. 16. 23. T. A.
Pariſiis.

Figura Revolutionis Lunæ.
332. 41

1646.
Aprilis
D. H. M.
24. 20. 0. T. A.
Pariſiis.

Figura Electionis Temporis.
333. 52.

1646.
Maji
D. H. M.
8. 19. 9. T. A.
Pariſiis.

[The figures above are the Horoscope of Count Chavigny, his 1646 Solar Revolution, his Lunar Revolution preceding the Journey, and the Election chart for the Journey.]

[The dates and times are 28 March 1608 at 11:23 PM, 29 March 1646 at 4:23 AM, 25 April 1646 at 8:00 AM, and 9 May 1646 at 7:09 AM.]

[However, the Electional figure is not accurately drawn! It looks like he calculated the chart for 8 May instead of 9 May. The House cusps are approximately correct, but on 9 May the Moon was actually in 3♓19 (not in 21♒), Mercury in 9♊11, Venus in 2♉50 Rx, Mars in 11♈28, Jupiter in 4♋29, and Saturn in 8♉56.]

Moreover, in the year 1645, in the beginning of the Revolution of the Year, or the revolution of the Sun, the significator of the MC and of actions and dignities was being directed to 8 Scorpio sextile Mars, presaging labors, travels, and dignity. And then he was made Plenipotentiary for General Peace, and he prepared everything for a long journey to Münster, a city of Germany, where all the Plenipotentiaries of the Princes were convened; but by an altered royal decree or a decree of the Prime Minister someone else was sent.

Moreover, in the year 1646, to the aforesaid direction, which had not yet allotted its own effect, there is added the direction of Mercury ruler of the 9th to the partile sextile of Jupiter Ruler of the ASC. Both of which were strong indicators of journeys. And so that direction signified a long and fortunate journey. But the solar revolution of that same year was also presaging the same thing. For in it the radical place of Venus was in the ASC, Mercury and the Sun rulers of the 9th were in the 1st with Mars ruler of the 9th of the revolution, Mars and Mercury conjoined in opposition to the Moon, which had returned to its own radical place under the rulership of Mercury, and the Moon was in trine to Venus ruler of the 3rd and to Saturn Ruler of the ASC. Moreover, Jupiter, Ruler of the MC and the 9th,[1] was in the 4th in mutual reception by domicile with Mercury, and trine the ASC. All of which were presaging a long and auspicious journey, so that already from the beginning of the revolution I had predicted the same thing to the most illustrious Lord.

But in the lunar revolution which preceded the day of departure, the Moon was the Ruler of the ASC in trine to the Sun ruler of the 9th of the radix and to Saturn ruler of the 9th of that revolution, then in trine to Venus, and to its (the Moon's) ruler Mercury, with which it was in mutual reception by exaltation. Moreover, Jupiter was in the ASC under the rulership of the Moon and in its sextile;

---

[1] 27 Scorpio is on the cusp of the 9th, but half of Sagittarius is in the 9th, so Morin took Jupiter to be co-ruler of the 9th.

and it was exalted there and the Ruler of the MC, and in almost partile trine to it; but it was also in sextile to the Sun and Saturn, rulers of the 9th of the radix and the 9th of this revolution. By which concourse of the benefics, nothing more fortunate could be selected for a long and auspicious journey, which this revolution was also presaging manifestly [see page 83].

Moreover, in the figure for the Election of the time of departure, which was briefly standing firm, prudence was conjoined with astrological science. For since the departure had to be by day, I didn't want the Sun to be in the first house, because Saturn and Mars would also have been in the 1st or in the 12th. And consequently they would also have portended illnesses for the most illustrious Lord, and also in its 12th misfortunes for his servants and horses, from which I was keen to make those servants and horses immune, in so far as those things were pertaining to the most illustrious Lord himself. And also I did not want the malefics to be in the 10th, 9th, or 8th, because they would have portended unlucky things for the actions and dignities of that same Lord as well as for his journey; and in the 8th at least dangers to his life.

And so I preferred the Sun, Saturn, Venus, and Mars to be in the 11th, with Mars strong and oriental going ahead in doryphory to the Sun. And I fortified the ASC for the fortunate health of that most illustrious Lord, and the MC for a fortunate success of his undertakings—in fact putting the exalted Jupiter in the ASC, which was the ruler of his radical ASC, and putting it in trine to the MC which it was ruling, and both the ASC and the MC in sextile to Venus which ruled the Sun and Saturn. Moreover, I put the Moon Ruler of the ASC in the 9th house for the journey above the radical place of Venus,[1] which in this figure was in its own domicile; and Mercury was alone well disposed in the 12th, which was not able to be harmful. These were therefore fortunately placed, for although the 8th cusp of the radix was rising on the ASC, neverthe-

---

[1] But alas, the Moon was not in 21♒ conjunct the radical Venus in 24♒, but it was actually in 3♓19! However, there it was in close trine to Jupiter on the cusp of the ASC—a very favorable aspect.

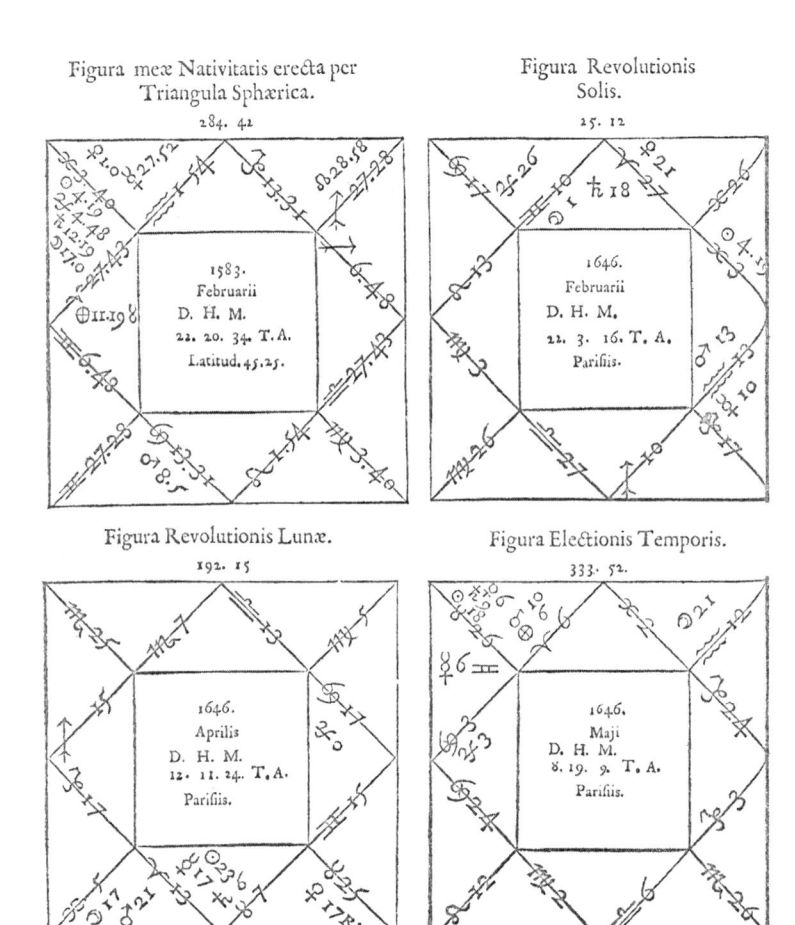

Figura meæ Nativitatis erecta per
Triangula Sphærica.
284. 41

1583.
Februarii
D. H. M.
22. 20. 34. T. A.
Latitud. 45. 25.

Figura Revolutionis
Solis.
25. 12

1646.
Februarii
22. 3. 16. T. A.
Parisiis.

Figura Revolutionis Lunæ.
192. 15

1646.
Aprilis
D. H. M.
12. 11. 24. T. A.
Parisiis.

Figura Electionis Temporis.
333. 52.

1646.
Maji
D. H. M.
8. 19. 9. T. A.
Parisiis.

[The figures above are the Horoscope of J. B. Morin, his 1646 Solar Revolution, his Lunar Revolution preceding the Journey, and the Election chart for the Journey.]

[The dates and times are 23 February 1583 at 8:34 AM, 22 February 1646 at 3:16 PM, 12 April 1646 at 11:24 PM, and 9 May 1646 at 7:09 AM.]

[The Electional figure is not accurately drawn! The House cusps are approximately correct, but the Moon was actually in 3♓19 (not in 21♒), Mercury in 9♊11, Venus in 2♉50 Rx, Mars in 11♈28, Jupiter in 4♋29, and Saturn in 8♉56.]

less Jupiter in the ASC was stronger and was preserving his health and life. And there was only something to be feared from false friends on account of Saturn and Mars in the 11th, which were not able to cause minor inconveniences else where, and which spared that sort of effect is said below.

But now in the solar revolution, the ASC on the day of departure—namely the 9th of May—had come by its annual direction to the 16th degree of the 8th house partile Venus in the revolution itself, which was the ruler of the 3rd and strong. Moreover the Sun had come to 12 ♊, a place square the Moon of both the radix and the revolution.

But in the lunar revolution, the MC in the hour of departure was being directed to 6 ♍—that is, on that very day it was coming to the radical place of the Moon. And the ASC by direction had come to 19 ♏—that is, on that very day it had come to the square of the radical Venus; and the Moon had come to 12 ♓ opposite its radical place, and sextile Venus and Mercury in that same revolution. Therefore on that day there was a very great consensus of the stars for a fortunate and lucky journey.

Moreover, since in the Election of the time for that journey, I had also decided to have a reason for myself. Now it must be seen whether I had also provided properly for that.

Therefore, in my nativity Jupiter and Saturn rulers of the 9th, then Mercury and the Moon rulers of the 3rd, with Mars ruler of the ASC centrally located in the 3rd, were significators of journeys; but especially Jupiter ruler of the cusp of the 9th, which was ruling all the planets except Mercury, to which its was nevertheless conjunct.[1] Moreover, in the year 1646 at the beginning of the annual revolution, the radical MC had come by direction to 16 ♓ almost the place of the Moon, which was conjoined to Jupiter and Saturn; and it was therefore the significator of journeys. And the

---

[1] By a wide "heads and tails" aspect, since Mercury was in 27♒52 and Jupiter was in 4♓48.

Part of Fortune in the 1st had come to 17♋ precisely trine the Moon herself. These configurations therefore also presaged a journey for me.

Moreover, in the annual solar revolution, a long journey was also being strongly signified. For the ASC of the radix was in the MC of the revolution, which was signifying new undertakings and actions for me. Venus, moreover, ruler of the 10th[1] was in the 9th applying to the radical ASC, and it was sextile Jupiter the ruler of the cusp of the 9th, and trine the ASC, which was certainly by no means obscurely presaging a long journey. Furthermore, Mars Ruler of Venus and the MC was on the cusp of the 7th with Mercury in Aquarius, which signified not only labors but also Mercurial contentions, which I had after my return with Fromm the Regius Professor of Mathematics at Copenhagen for the *Restoral of Astronomy*, and with P. Leonardo Duliris for his Resumé of my *Finding of Longitudes,* against whom I wrote in that year.[2]

But in the monthly lunar revolution closely preceding the 9th of May, a journey was also strongly signified. For the Moon was square the ASC, and its antiscion was culminating, and the Moon itself was in the 3rd with Mars, which was partly the Ruler of the 3rd and the 10th; then the Sun, and Mercury which was the ruler of the 9th and trine the ASC. Moreover, Jupiter the Ruler of the ASC was in the beginning of Cancer under the rulership of the Moon itself, which in turn it ruled, and it was separating from a trine of the radical Mercury to a trine of the radical Venus and a cluster of planets. All these things were therefore greatly indicating a long journey.

But already in the Electional figure, what could I do more fortunately for me than to put Jupiter the ruler of the cusp of the 9th in my nativity, and of almost all of the planets, in the ASC and trine its own radical place and that cluster of planets, and to put in the

---

[1] Taurus was intercepted in the 10th, so Morin takes it to be a co-ruler of the 10th.
[2] These are references to two books that Morin wrote and to two men who wrote critical reviews of them.

85

MC the place of that same cluster of planets that Jupiter was ruling and which it was fortifying by its own partile trine. But the Moon Ruler of the ASC and Jupiter in the 9th in the place[1] of the radical Mercury and afflicted by a malefic[2]? These things were certainly very artfully disposed for a journey that was also very lucky.

Furthermore, in the solar revolution, the MC was being directed on the 9th of May to 9♋ the radical place of Mars in the 3rd and trine the cluster of my planets; moreover, the Sun at 1♉ was sextile the radical Venus; and the Moon at 20♋ was square Venus in that revolution.

But in the lunar revolution, the MC had come to 0♎ square Jupiter in that revolution, the ASC to 5♐ square the cluster of my planets, and especially the Sun and Saturn; moreover the Sun had come to Libra[3] square the radical Mars; and the Moon to 4♓ the radical place of the Sun and Jupiter and the cluster of Planets. All of which was also suitable for a long and lucky journey. And having also inspected these in the year 64 of my age, I committed myself to this long journey in the summertime. And the Sun in the 8th of the annual revolution and which Ruled the ASC did not deter me, nor did Mars on the cusp of the 7th—namely, because in my radix no lethal direction would be completed in that year, and the rest of the directions were fortunate. Nevertheless, for my greater security, avoiding the heat of the Sun and the weariness of body, in [staying] quiet and [exercising] moderation as much as I could in banquets, I looked after my health, and I took caution lest I should fall into any illness.

Moreover, what was the result of all of the above said things? From the City of Paris to Lyons the travel was by land. From Lyons to Avignon by water—the whole company of men and

---

[1] But the Moon was not in 21♒, but in 4♓.

[2] I suppose he is referring to the antiscion of Saturn in 9♉, which would have been in 21♒ in partile conjunction with his false position of the Moon.

[3] The printed text has the symbol for the Moon's South Node by mistake for the symbol for Libra.

horses—and in that same passage we were transported on the Rhone in three larger boats. And finally from Avignon to Antibes we proceeded by land through the roughest places and mountains by horse, and [those places were] especially most difficult and dangerous to pass through.

Moreover, during the whole journey the most illustrious Lord was received with the honors due to a French Minister, to the intelligence, learning, skill in royal court matters, and to his great fame; and not here and there falling short on social obligations. And yet, not withstanding the change in climate, the summer heat of the Sun in Provence, the vines after the City of Lyons that are thicker and more productive [of wine] than those in Burgundy and France, which no one and especially none of the servants was sparing (because everywhere by custom they were offered copiously to the most illustrious Lord), so that not even one servant on foot, and not one horse had a bad time on the whole journey. For because anyone looking at the most illustrious Lord de Chavigny—[could see that] he in his way of life was the most moderate of men; and he most prudently governed his own health, whence it was no wonder that he was always in good health. And so with notable liveliness and with the sky always serene from the City of Paris we arrived at Antibes, where we dwelled for a month with the great heat of the Sun, but with no one—neither man nor horse suffering harm.

When a month had passed and the business affairs had been completed, the most illustrious Lord wanted to return to Paris, and I asked him that because the Election of the time made by me at Paris visualized an outstanding experiment, would he like [me] again to elect an hour to depart from Antibes. And so, when he had approved, and with everything carefully considered, I elected 4:27 AM on July 2nd. And again when everything had been prepared for departure at that moment, the most illustrious Lord waited with me in his room with the windows open to the east until be spied the rising of the Sun; and then without any delay he departed along with all his company, in his carriage, with horses and much baggage having been sent ahead by sea on account of the roughness and difficulty of the mountains, which would occur on the second day of the journey.

Furthermore, in the annual revolution of that most illustrious Lord, the ASC was then being directed to 14♋ square the radical Mercury ruler of the 9th house, and the Moon was in the 9th of the radix. But the MC was being directed to 17♓ sextile Venus in that same revolution between the bodies of Mars and Mercury that were conjoined in the 1st, of which Mercury was the ruler of the 9th of the radix, and Mars was the ruler of the 9th of the revolution.

Moreover, in the figure of the lunar revolution most closely preceding the 2nd of July, the place of the radical Mars is ascending, which planet is ruling the 9th in the solar revolution, and the 10th in this revolution. Moreover, Venus is the ruler of the 9th almost partilely conjunct Saturn the Ruler of the ASC to which she is applying. And Mars is in her own domicile and angular in the 4th; and Saturn, Venus, and Mars were in trine to the ASC and to the Moon. All of which things were strongly presaging a journey and also a lucky one, because Jupiter was sextile Mars, Venus, and Saturn and trine the MC. Moreover, the Moon and the Sun were also favoring the MC with fortunate aspects. And although they were in bad houses, nevertheless they were not being afflicted by the malefics. Besides, in this revolution, the ASC on the 2nd of July was being directed to 11♌ sinister trine the Sun, Mercury, and Jupiter in the radix. But the MC was being directed to the places of Mars, Venus, and Saturn of that revolution; but the Moon was being directed to the places of Mars and Jupiter in the solar revolution.

But in my annual revolution, the MC had come on the 2nd of July to 1♍ opposite Venus and the cluster of my planets; the ASC was being directed to 15♏ trine the radical Moon and the cluster of planets; and the Sun was being directed to 11♊ square that same cluster.

Moreover, in the figure of my Lunar Revolution that most closely preceded the 2nd of July 1646. The Moon is under the Earth by day and angular in the 4th, the ruler of the 9th, trine the

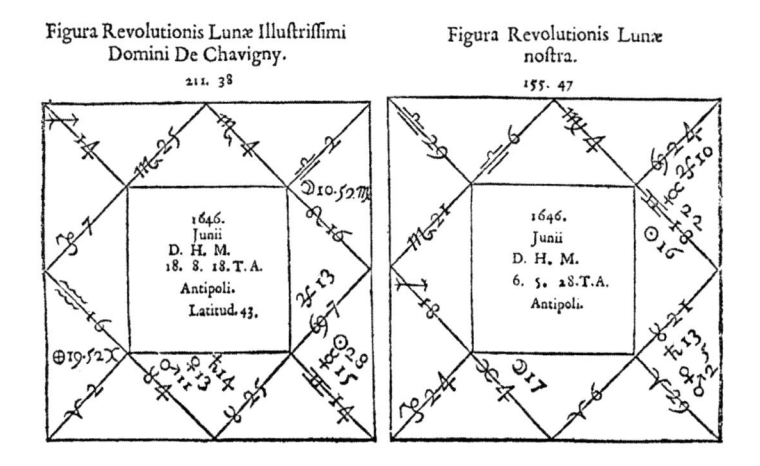

Figura Revolutionis Lunæ Illustrissimi
Domini De Chavigny.
211. 38

Figura Revolutionis Lunæ
nostra.
155. 47

[The figures above are the Lunar Revolution of Count Chavigny, and the Lunar Revolution of Morin—both of them preceding the start of the return from the Journey,]

[The dates and times are 18 June 1646 at 8:18 PM, and 6 June 1646 at 5:28 PM., both of them set for Antibes, France]

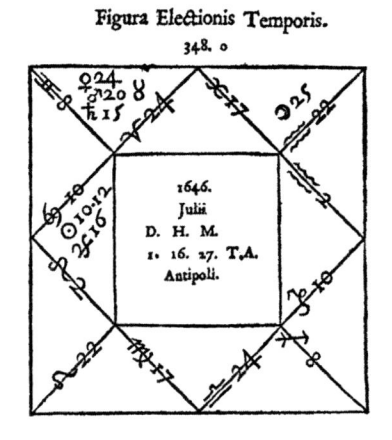

Figura Electionis Temporis.
348. 0

[The figure of the Election for the Departure from Antibes set for 2 July 1646 at Sunrise 4:27 AM]

ASC and Jupiter ruler of the 1st,[1] with whom she is mutual reception by domicile, and she is also square the Sun the ruler of the 9th,[2] and Mercury Ruler of the MC. Moreover, Mars Ruler of the ASC is conjunct the powerful Venus, which is trine the MC. All of which are rightly related to a journey. In addition, neither the Sun, the Moon, the ASC, nor the MC, were afflicted by the malefics. Besides, in this revolution the ASC was being directed monthly to 2 July at the hour of the departure, when it was at 27♎ opposite my radical ASC, and running forward on that day to the trine of my cluster of planets. And the Moon at 18♒ arriving on that same day to the cluster itself. And the Sun on that same day arriving at 2♉ square that same cluster. And so from the stars there were many stimuli.

But with these being thus, I elected the hour mentioned above, when the *Caelum* and the planets, with the exception of the Sun, were nicely disposed in the 1st of the Electional figure, which since it would have turned out best, should I have turned this away? Therefore in this figure the Sun and the ASC are applying to Jupiter, which in return is exalted in the ASC, and trine the MC which it rules; and again the Moon, ruler of the ASC, the Sun, and Jupiter is in the 9th on the radical place of Venus in the figure of the most illustrious Lord. Moreover again, Mars, and Venus are in the 11th—namely, because I wanted them to be away from the 1st, 12th, 10th, 9th, and 8th houses on account of the reasons stated above. And the Sun and Jupiter were in square to their own radical places [in the figure] of the most illustrious Lord. But that which [in this Electional figure] relates to me, is that the ASC is in trine to the cluster of my planets, and Jupiter the ruler of my radical 9th is in the ASC; and the radical place of my Moon was partilely on the MC; and the Moon herself was in the place of my radical Mercury and sextile the radical ASC, while applying to the cluster of planets.

---

[1] Jupiter is co-ruler of the ASC, since the cusp is 21 ♏, but ♐ is in the 1st house.
[2] The Sun is the co-ruler of the 9th, since 24♋ is on the cusp but ♌ is in the 9th house.

Now, this is what came about from this. From the City of Antibes to Lyons the travel was on land. But then the most illustrious Lord, his own carriage, and the greater part of his own company passed on through Burgundy, but he himself—with most of his company on foot—wanted to go down the Loire with some special and more necessary domestics; but with an intolerable condition existing over the river, he was forced by the fear of illness to go down the river at Nevers, and to finish off the rest of the journey by riding; and we all arrived at Paris healthy and cheerful at the beginning of August.

And none of us, neither man nor horse fell ill on the whole journey, during the time when in many places both men and pack animals were dying from too much heat and dryness; and in the cities with abundant water, we were finding men from villages three or four leagues distant who had come with carts and large jars seeking water for men and pack animals. So that [when we had arrived] at Paris, we aroused much admiration because in all that journey of three months no man or horse had had any illness.

But finally, it must be stated what Saturn and Mars did in the 11th house of that Election. They did indeed arouse false, malign, and fraudulent enemies, who, in the absence of the most illustrious Lord Count, worked with all their powers to evict him from his Ministry; and it was believed that this was going to happen here and there in the Court at Fontainebleau. And so he was warned by friends, that he should turn away from the Court and go to Paris. I am rather silent about the false pretexts that were received, among which however was this—that the most illustrious Lord had taken an astrologer with him to consult about the life of the King,[1] the Queen,[2] the Most Eminent Cardinal Mazarin,[3] the Prime Minister

---
[1] Louis XIV (1638-1715), who was only 8 in 1646.
[2] Anne of Austria (1601-1666), who was the regent of France 1643-1651) and a close friend of Cardinal Mazarin, whom she appointed Prime Minister in 1643.
[3] Giulio Mazzarini, called in French Jules Mazarin (1602-1661), He was created Cardinal in 1641, and as Prime Minister from 1643 to his death, he was very powerful in France.

of France, etc. But concerning which, certainly not a single word was spoken during the whole time of the journey.

Moreover, from this envy and slander it resulted that the most illustrious Lord also asked me twice whether I could see in the stars any misfortune in dignities that was threatening him? And I always said that there was nothing threatening. Nevertheless, because some days had also passed since our return, but he had not yet seen his Eminence the Cardinal, nor therefore the Queen.[1] I said that it would be good if he would not go and see the Cardinal at any random hour, but rather at an elected one! For Christ himself, being warned by the Apostles, that He should not go to Jerusalem on account of the Jews wanting to kill him, replied not without cause, "Are there not twelve hours in the day?"—namely, some safe, some lucky, and others dangerous or unlucky."

Consequently, if he would let me elect an appropriate hour that would be favorable, I elected the following hour, in which the sign of the 10th of the radix[2] was ascending, and its ruler Venus applies to the Moon[3] which was powerful and the Ruler of the MC. Moreover the 10th house, which is the House of Dignities, is very fortunate. For the Sun and Jupiter, which were significators of honors in the 4th of the radix, were in the 10th itself—the Sun in its own domicile, and Jupiter exalted. Moreover, Mercury the Ruler of the MC of the radix was with the Heart of Leo on the cusp of the 11th.[4] Mars ruler of the 7th was sextile the Sun and trine the ASC. Moreover, the Moon and Venus were sextile the Part of Fortune, which was found in the place of the radical Moon. And although the Sun was square Saturn (for we cannot have everything the way we would like), nevertheless the Sun was in the 10th and strong—namely, in its own sign.

---

[1] Cardinal Mazarin actually controlled access to the Queen.
[2] 29 ♍ was on the cusp of the Count's MC, but most of the house was occupied by the sign ♎.
[3] Actually, the Moon is separating from Venus and applying to the MC.
[4] This was the fixed star Regulus or α Leonis, which was in 24♌23 at the time of the Count's birth.

Whence I dared to assert that if he would visit the Cardinal in that hour—the 10th house being so favorable—I could not persuade myself that he would not be received favorably, and that there would then be nothing to fear. And certainly the matter turned out like that.

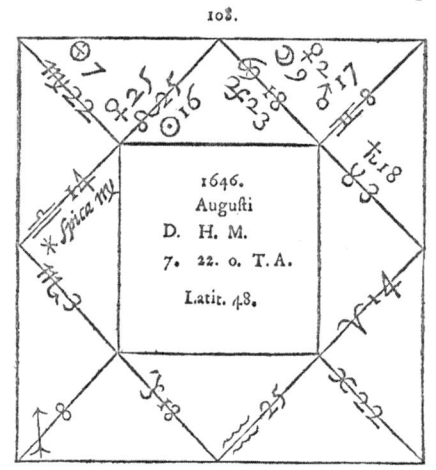

Figura Electionis Temporis ex sola genesis Figura.
108.

1646.
Augusti
D. H. M.
7. 22. 0. T.A.
Latit. 48.

[Figure of the Election of a Time from just the Figure of a Nativity]
[In the 11th House it should be Mercury in 25 Leo, not Venus.]
[Set for Fontainebleau, France 8 August 1646 at 10:00 AM]

For by my warning on the day before, he went to Fontainebleau and by night lest he be seen. Then on the following morning at the elected hour he visited the Cardinal with fortunate results, by whose company he was received, and at lunch he was taken to the Queen, by whom he was also well received. In the hour of the Council he was ordered to take his seat in his second Ministry. And not in these things indeed did he need to employ the work of a Magnate, in which matter he was priding himself, not without admiration.

I could introduce many other Elections here from my own practices and those of others that have met with outstanding and hoped for success. But (as is plain) it would be too long to explain them; and consequently, let those shown above suffice. And here we shall bring to an end our Theory of Astrology [dedicated] to the honor and glory of the Eternal Wisdom of our Lord Jesus Christ, who made the Heaven and the Earth and enriched the heavenly bodies with admirable virtues. And let there be eternal Praise, Virtue, and Glory to Him. Amen.

THE END

APPENDIX 1

The time used in all of the charts in Book 26 is Local Apparent Time (LAT). To assist the reader who may want to recalculate some of the charts, I have prepared a table of the Equation of Time for the year 1625. That year is approximately in the middle of the time period spanned by the charts. The Equation of Time changes slowly from year to year, but the table shown below is sufficiently accurate for dates within 75 years or more before or after 1625.

The argument of the table is the true longitude of the Sun. To find the value of the Equation of Time locate the solar longitude that is just before the longitude of the Sun and the one just after; these are at 5 degree intervals. Interpolate these two values to get the value for an intermediate longitude. Once found, the Equation of Time can be rounded off to the nearest whole minute.

Table of the Equation of Time for the Year 1625

Sun	Eq.T	Sun	EqT	Sun	EqT	Sun	Eq.T
0	+7.7	90	+0.9	180	-7.7	270	-0.9
5	+6.1	95	+2.0	185	-9.4	275	+1.6
10	+4.5	100	+3.0	190	-11.0	280	+4.0
15	+2.9	105	+4.0	195	-12.4	285	+6.3
20	+1.4	110	+4.8	200	-13.7	290	+8.4
25	-0.0	115	+5.3	205	-14.7	295	+10.2
30	-1.3	120	+5.6	210	-15.4	300	+11.8
35	-2.3	125	+5.7	215	-15.9	305	+13.1
40	-3.2	130	+5.5	220	-16.1	310	+14.1
45	-3.8	135	+5.0	225	-15.9	315	+14.7

50	-4.2	140	+4.3	230	-15.4	320	+15.0
55	-4.3	145	+3.3	235	-14.5	325	+14.9
60	-4.1	150	+2.1	240	-13.3	330	+14.6
65	-3.7	155	+0.7	245	-11.8	335	+13.9
70	-3.1	160	-0.8	250	-10.0	340	+13.0
75	-2.3	165	-2.5	255	-7.9	345	+11.9
80	-1.3	170	-4.2	260	-5.7	350	+10.6
85	-0.2	175	-5.9	265	-3.3	355	+9.2
90	+0.9	180	-7.7	270	-0.9	360	+7.7

LMT = LAT + Equation of Time
LAT = LMT - Equation of Time

Suppose for example that the Sun in a chart is in 23°19' of Scorpio. This is equivalent to 233°19' or 233.3° to the nearest tenth of a degree. Looking in the table, we find for 230° that the Equation of Time has the value -15.4, and for 235° the value is -14.5. The difference is 0.9 and it is decreasing. We want 3.3/5 or 0.67 of that difference; it will be 0.67 X 0.9 or 0.6., so we subtract that amount from the figure for 230°, and we have –15.4 reduced by 0.6 or -14.8. That is the value in minutes and tenths of a minute. We can round it off, and we will say that the approximate value of the Equation of Time is 15 minutes. Then, if the stated time was 6:05 AM LAT, the equivalent LMT will be 6:05 AM -0:15 or 5:50 AM LMT.

Index of Persons.

ᶜAlî ibn abi al-Rijâl, *astrologer* 5,8,9,11,15,16,19,20,27,28,51,52
Al-Kindî, Abû Yûsuf, *science writer* 15n.2,101
Angelis, Alexander de, *cleric* 61,66,101
Arabs, *astrologers* 3,5,6,9,11,14-20,20-30,31-32
Bourdin, Nicolas, Marquis de Villennes 58n.1,101
Bishops 72
Bouthillier, Léon, Count of Chavigny (*See* Chavigny)
Carmody, Francis, *scholar* 101
Cardan, Jerome, *astrologer* 5,38-43,49,55,66-69, 101
Ceresario, Paride, *astrologer* 68
Chaldeans, *astrologers* 16,32
Chancellors 72
Chavigny, Léon de Bouthillier, Count 78,79,80,87,89
Chief Officers 72
Christians 33,34
Cicero, Marcus Tullius, *writer* xi
Coley, Henry, *astrologer* 101
Commanders 59
Devil vii,31,32,33,37,45
Dorotheus, *astrologer* 19
Duliris, P. Leonardo, *scholar* 85
Elizabeth, Biblical character 64
Farnese, Alessandro, Pope Paul III 68n.1

Firmicus Maternus, Julius, *astrologer* vii,3n.1
Fromm, *professor of mathematics* 85
Gauls 6
Generals 41,42,72
Germans 36
God 20,31,32,43,55,60,77
Gustavus Adolphus, King of Sweden 58
Haly (*See* [<]Alî ibn abi al-Rijâl)
Hermes Trismegistus, *astrologer* 8,9,15,22,102
Indians, *astrologers* 3,7,8,14,32
Jesus Christ 94
Kidd, Douglas Alexander, *lexicographer* iii,102
King of China
King of France 38,56
Kings 41,42,43,44,49,57,58,59
Liechtenstein, Peter, *publisher* 15n.2,103
Lilly, William, *astrologer* ix,102
Louis XII, King of France 91n.1
Luke, *Gospel writer* 64
Magnates 17,57,58,68,72,77,93
Maria Giacopo, *astrologer* 68
Mashâ[>]âllâh, *astrologer* 17n.1
Mazarin, Jules, Cardinal 78,91,92n.1
Messahala (*See* Mashâ[>]âllâh)
Ministers 57,59,87
Morin, Jean Baptiste, astrologer vii,viii,ix,x,xi,xii,102,103
Omar Tiberiades, *astrologer* 6-8,103
Oriental Peoples, *astrologers* 14,31
Partridge & Blunden, *publishers* ix,102
Plenipotentiaries 81
Pontano, Giovanni, *astrologer* 14,103

Prime Ministers 57,59,81
Princes 42,49,52,56,57,58,68,72,81
Ptolemy, Claudius, *science writer* vii,ixn.1,3,5,6,7,24n.1,25, 32n.3,39,47n.1,58n.1
Queen of France (Anne of Austria) 91n.2
Queens 72,77
Ratdolt, Erhard, *publisher* 101
Schöner, Johann, *astrologer* 70,71
Sforza, Ludovico, Duke of Milan 55
Spaniards 36
Thorndike, Lynn, *historian* 68n.1,103
Tooke & Sawbridge, *publishers* 15n.1,102
Vlacq, Adrian, *publisher* 103
Virgin Mary 64
Vuellius (*See* Vettius Valens)
Vettius Valens, *astrologer* 8n.1,29n.1,103

Bibliography.

ʿAlî ibn abi al-Rijâl, Abû'l Hasan
Liber completus de iudiciis astrorum.
Venice: Erhard Ratdolt, 1485.

Al-Kindî
De iudiciis astrorum
[The Judgments of the Stars]
Venice: Peter Liechtenstein, 1509.

Angelis, Alexander de
In Astrologos coniectores.
(Conjectures against the Astrologers]
Lyons: H. Cardon, 1615. 4to xxviii,351,xxxi pp.
Rome: B. Zanetti, 1615. 2nd ed. 4to

Bourdin, Nicolas, Marquis de Villennes
Le Centilogve de Ptolomee.
Paris: Cardin Besongne, 1651.

Cardan, Jerome
Opera Omnia
Lyons: Huguetan & Ravaud, 1663. 10 vols.
New York & London: Johnson Reprint, 1967. 10 vols.

Carmody, Francis J.
Arabic astronomical and astrological Sciences
in Latin Translation.
Berekeley & Los Angeles: Univ. of California Press, 1956.

Coley, Henry
Clavis Astrologiae Elimata.
London: Tooke & Sawbridge, 1676.

Hermes
Centiloquy.
translated by James Herschel Holden in
Five Medieval Astrologers.
Tempe, Az.: A.F.A., Inc., 2008.

Holden, James Herschel (translator)
Five Medieval Astrologers.
Tempe. Az.: A.F.A., Inc., 2008.

A History of Horoscopic Astrology
Tempe, Az.: A.F.A., Inc., 1996. 1st ed.
Tempe, Az.: A.F.A., Inc., 2006. 2nd rev ed

Kidd, Douglas Alexander
Collins Latin-English English-Latin Dictionary.
London & Glasgow: Collins, 1972.

Lilly, William
Christian Astrology, Modestly
Treated of in three Books.
London: John Partridge and Humphrey Blunden, 1647.

Lull, Ramón
Book Explaining the Elemental Figures of the Demonstrative Art.

Morin, Jean Baptiste
Astrologicarum domorum cabala detecta a Joanne Baptista Morino.
Paris: J. Moreau, 1623.

Remarques Astrologiques.

Paris: P. Ménard, 1657.
Paris: Retz, 1976. repr.

Astrologica Gallica.
The Hague: A. Vlacq, 1661.

Omar Tiberiades
De nativitatibus.
trans. by John of Seville
Venice: Sessa, 1503.

Pontano, Giovanni Gioviano
Centiloquium.
Venice, 1503.

Thorndike, Lynn
A History of Magic and Experimental Science (HMES)
New York: Columbia University Press, 1923-1958. 8 vols.

Various Authors
Liber novem iudicium.
The Book of Nine Judges.
Venice: Peter Liechtenstein, 1509.

Vettius Valens
Anthologiae.
ed. D. Pingree
Leipzig: B. G. Teubner, 1986.

Printed by BoD in Norderstedt, Germany